TREES, FRUITS & FLOWERS OF THE BIBLE

OF THE BIBLE

A GUIDE FOR BIBLE READERS AND NATURALISTS

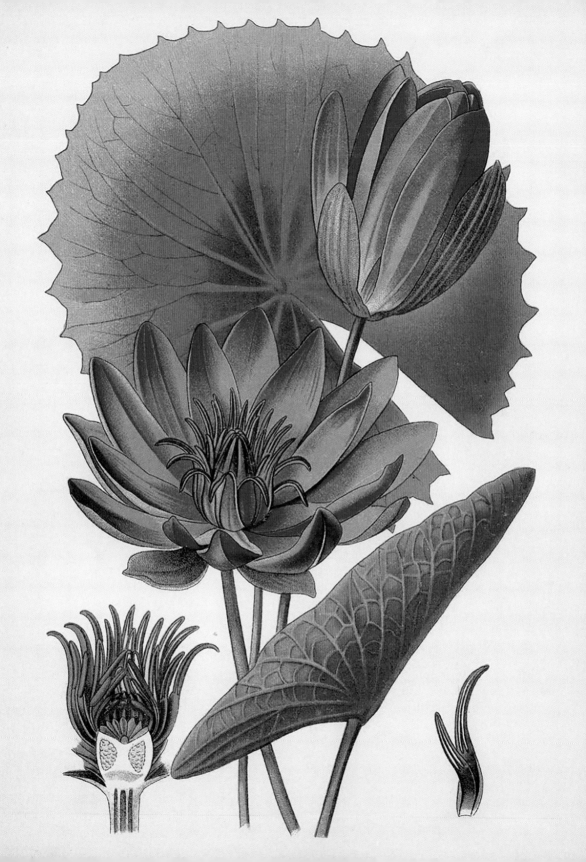

TREES, FRUITS & FLOWERS OF THE BIBLE

A GUIDE FOR BIBLE READERS AND NATURALISTS

PETER GOODFELLOW
WITH MARIANNE TAYLOR

JOHN BEAUFOY PUBLISHING

First published in the United Kingdom in 2021 by John Beaufoy Publishing,
11 Blenheim Court, 316 Woodstock Road, Oxford OX2 7NS, England
www.johnbeaufoy.com

10 9 8 7 6 5 4 3 2 1

ISBN 978-1-912081-36-3

Printed and bound in Malaysia by Times Offset (M) Sdn. Bhd.

Project management by Rosemary Wilkinson
Cartography by William Smuts
Designed and typeset by Gulmohur Press, New Delhi

PAGE 2: EGYPTIAN WATER LILY; PAGE 3 BLACK AND WHITE GRAPES

CONTENTS

'IN THE BEGINNING'

O ur trip through the Bible, via the plant life found within its pages, needs to begin with a few words about our destination – the Holy Land. Not everyone will be able to visit this landscape in person, but some mental picture of the general environment and its habitats will help give us a sense of place, so that the scripture references to cedars or thorns or olives are more than just names on a page.

A glance at a map shows that the landscape of the Bible is confined to a narrow zone in the south-east corner of the Mediterranean Sea. Since ancient times Palestine (or Canaan, as it was called before that) has been a corridor of lush land between the more arid and inhospitable expanse of inland Arabia and the Mediterranean Sea. It was an ideal route for traders travelling between Egypt and Asia Minor, and for the armies of leaders in the quest to enlarge their empires. It was a territory that was often fought over by rival nations, and is still troubled by conflict today.

When Moses led the Israelites out of Egypt, they wandered in the desert for 40 years until they came within sight of the land that God had promised them. Here God told Moses he could not cross the river to enter the Promised Land; instead he led him to the 'top of Pisgah [to] look west and north and south and east' (Deuteronomy ch. 3, v. 27). Pisgah, or Mount Nebo, is in the northern part of the land known as Moab, on the northeastern corner of the Dead Sea. From this elevated vantage point, Moses could see all the land his people would inherit, and from here we can get a sense of the wide variety of countryside that the events of the Bible take place in: mountains, forest, farmland, water, desert and human habitation.

The land we are reading about does not fit neatly into a modern political map. Although for many years the Jews lived in Egypt and Babylon, most of their story takes place in 'Palestine', and this is now covered by two modern nations, Israel and Jordan. Due to the politics of the area today, many people are sensitive about who has the right to various parts of this land, so in the pages that follow 'Palestine' means the land in the Bible story; 'Jordan' refers to the river or the valley that bears its name, and 'Israel' refers to the ancient name of the Jewish kingdom, which lay north of Jerusalem, as opposed to Judah, which lay to the south, unless it is clearly stated otherwise.

It is the mountains that shape the lands of the Bible, the Holy Land as Christians call it, that

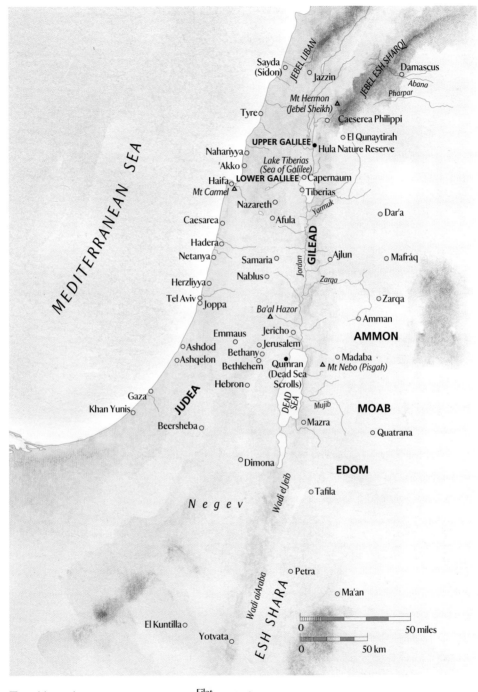

Sayda
(Sidon)

JEBEL LIBAN

Jazzin

JEBEL ESH SHARQI

Damascus

Abana

Pharpar

Mt Hermon
(Jebel Sheikh)

Tyre

Caeserea Philippi

El Qunaytirah

UPPER GALILEE

Hula Nature Reserve

Nahariyya

*Lake Tiberias
(Sea of Galilee)*

'Akko

Haifa

LOWER GALILEE

Capernaum

Mt Carmel

Tiberias

Nazareth

Yarmuk

Dar'a

Caesarea

Afula

GILEAD

Hadera

Netanya

Jordan

Ajlun

Mafráq

Samaria

Herzliyya

Nablus

Zarqa

Tel Aviv

Joppa

Zarqa

Ba'al Hazor

Amman

Emmaus

Jericho

AMMON

Ashdod

Jerusalem

Bethany

Ashqelon

Bethlehem

Madaba

Hebron

Qumran
(Dead Sea
Scrolls)

Mt Nebo (Pisgah)

MEDITERRANEAN SEA

Gaza

JUDEA

*DEAD
SEA*

Mujib

MOAB

Khan Yunis

Beersheba

Mazra

Quatrana

Dimona

EDOM

N e g e v

Wadi el Jeib

Tafila

Wadi al Araba

Petra

E S H   S H A R A

Ma'an

0				50 miles

0				50 km

El Kuntilla

Yotvata

THE HOLY LAND

Eilat   Aqaba

lie along the eastern shore of the Mediterranean Sea. Near the coast two parallel ranges of mountains run from north to south. The western range is unbroken from Mount Taurus (3,685 m/12,089 ft above sea level) in Asia Minor (in modern Turkey) in the Taurus Mountains overlooking Tarsus where St Paul was born, to Qornet es Saruda (3,087 m/10,127 ft above sea level) in Lebanon, which is capped in perpetual snow. From there, the uplands go into the districts north and south of Galilee, rising to Mount Carmel by the coast (actually part of a ridge 39 km/24 m long, 546 m/1,791 ft above sea level at its highest point), and the plateau-like hill country that includes Jerusalem (754 m/2,474 ft), Bethlehem (775 m/2,543 ft), Hebron (930 m/3,050 ft) and most of the historical sites of Palestine. South of here is the Negev, described as 'the wilderness' in, for example, 'The voice of one crying in the wilderness' (Isaiah ch. 40, v. 3 and St John ch. 1, v. 23), or 'the desert' in modern translations.

Here is a land that varies between the harsh, barren landscape of the south, to the land 'flowing with milk and honey' (Job, ch. 20, v. 17) west of the Jordan, to the majestic Mount Hermon in the north. For most of Palestine, geographers say the area has a Mediterranean climate. There is a marked dry season, beginning from mid-June and lasting until mid-September. During this time, the weather conditions day after day stay very much the same. Winds develop that can be quite strong at times, but are usually steady, so this is the dependable period in biblical times for shipping; winds in the rainy season are much more changeable and dangerous. Bad weather held sway when St Paul was being taken to Rome (Acts ch. 27), and Jesus calmed a severe winter storm on Galilee (St Mark ch. 4 and St Luke ch. 8). The winter rain is not very predictable, and significant rainfall may not occur until after Christmas.

The summers are hot. Average temperatures in the Jordan valley from May to October are usually well over 30° C/86° F. Winters are much cooler, with the temperature falling below 10° C/50° F in December to February; in Jerusalem the average August temperature is 29° C/85° F, whereas in January it is only 8° C/47° F. Frost may occur then at night, and there may even sometimes be snowfall in the south, as happened in the winter of 1991–1992, when banana plantations in Jericho were ruined. There are considerable local variations in temperature and rainfall through the area because of the landscape; the western-facing slopes see more rainfall than the eastern-facing slopes, and temperatures tend to increase the further you move away from the sea and further south.

As far as we know, Palestine has always had a coastline – indeed for millions of years the area was under the sea, which has resulted in much of the land now being formed of the maritime deposits of limestone, chalk and sandstone. Due to the wide variety of physical features, from snow-topped mountains to fertile plains to deserts, the natural vegetation of the land is very different from one area to another. Such a diverse landscape would have supported a rich and complex array of plants, which in turn would have provided food and shelter for all manner of animals. The Psalmist many years ago wrote 'the earth is full of your creatures' (Psalm 104, v. 24). This was certainly true in biblical times, when human activity had made relatively few inroads on the diverse natural habitats, even though the underlying rock was largely limestone or sandstone, except for the alluvial plain and Rift Valley.

At the eastern end of the Mediterranean Sea, from Anatolia in southern Turkey to southern Africa, runs the great Rift Valley. Some of the most diverse segments of habitat in it are the plains of Syria, Lebanon, Israel and Jordan, with the green belt of the Jordan River running through. This is the heart of the Holy Land and its flora and fauna. The lowlands behind the sand dunes of the coast are now orange groves, vineyards, and fields of cereals and vegetables, but in ancient times there would have been large areas of marshland as well as settlements. The hill country still has extensive areas of wild flowers in spring, providing a dazzling spectacle, and also supports shrubland comprising mainly dwarf oaks, carob trees and rockrose. This scrub can be very dense, particularly around Mount Carmel and on the

PLAINS OF JORDAN

CHRIST'S THORN

| TREES, FRUITS & FLOWERS OF THE BIBLE

hills around Galilee. The Rift Valley has vegetation as dense as a tropical jungle, and tropical levels of heat in summer to go with it. The heat and the water create a lush green ribbon of vegetation that closely follows the river. This zone consists primarily of tamarisk, which can grow to a height of 15 m (more than 45 ft). Another similarly sized tree, known as Christ's Thorn or Jujube (*Paliurus spina-christi*), also grows in Israel; its thorns are up to 2 cm (¾ in) long. Both of these tree species have been said to be the one used to make Christ's crown of thorns. Commentators believe the Jujube is the last tree mentioned in Jotham's parable in Judges ch. 9, vv.8–15.

The Negev Desert in the south is not a completely bare and sandy landscape as one might imagine; the hills may be unvegetated and stony, but many wadis (valleys that may have a stream running through them in the rainy season) and hollows have stunted bushes that survive the dry months, and a good rainy season will cause dormant seeds to germinate, bringing a flush of grass and flowers.

The climate, the contours of the landscape, and the patterns of human habitation through the centuries have resulted in there being several distinct and different plant communities in the region. The principal ones are:

Scrub and shrubland, called *garigue* and *maquis* respectively. The former has many soft-leaved, ground-layer plants, such as lavender, cistus, senecio, rosemary, thistles and wild thyme; the latter is a shrubland biome typically consisting of densely growing evergreens, such as holm oak, kermes oak, tree heath, strawberry tree, sage, juniper, buckthorn, spurge olive and myrtle.

Grassland.

Woodland of oak and pine, and **forests**, distinguished from woodland by having a fully closed canopy of mostly evergreen oaks and pines.

Cultivated land, managed (to a greater and lesser extent) to propagate crops from cereals to fruit trees, including both native and non-native species.

JUNIPER

CHAPTER |

TREES

Then God said, 'Let the land produce vegetation:
seed bearing plants and trees on the land that bear fruit
with seed in it, according to their various kinds.
≈ GENESIS
CH. 1, vv. 11-13
And it was so. The land produced vegetation:
plants bearing seeds according to their kinds and
trees bearing fruit with seed in it according to
their kinds. And there was evening,
and there was morning – the third day. ≈

When the Lord God made the earth and the heavens
– and no shrub of the field had yet appeared on the
earth and no plant of the fields had yet sprung up,
for the Lord God had not sent rain on the earth,
and there was no man to work the ground,
but streams came up from the earth and
watered the whole surface of the ground –
≈ GENESIS
CH. 2, vv. 4-9
the Lord God formed the man from the dust of the
ground and breathed into his nostrils the breath of life,
and the man became a living being.
Now the Lord God had planted a garden in the east,
in Eden, and there he put a man he had formed.
And the Lord God made all kinds of trees grow
out of the ground – trees that were pleasing
to the eye and good for food. ≈

These words were written perhaps 4,000 years ago, and form part of the Bible's description of the creation of the world. The creation story describes living things appearing in this order: fish and other marine animals, plants, most land animals, then birds in chapters 1 and 2 of Genesis. However, many believers today do accept the rather different version of events

Lebanon Cedar

that is evidenced by science. A range of scientists, including climatologists, geographers, zoologists and botanists, have also identified the Mediterranean basin as one of five regions in the world to have a distinct climate (see p. 8) and have documented the effect that this has on the area's natural flora. The botany of the Holy Land is indeed richly varied, from the wilderness of Beersheba in the south, to the top of Mount Hermon in the north. Scripture has many references to this, and modern travellers still remark, especially during pilgrimage time at Easter, on the beauty of the spring flowers.

About 3,000 species of Palestinian flora are known today, but the Bible mentions only about 130, mostly those that are useful or ornamental. Even then, relatively few species described in the Bible can be identified with certainty; a large proportion of the names are generic, such as nettles, briars and grass. It may seem frustrating to some readers, who are familiar with the detailed classification of plants to be found in modern field guides, to learn that the Bible refers simply to (1) *deshe*, signifying all low plants, (2) *'esebh*, including herbaceous plants; and (3) *'es peri*, embracing all trees (Genesis ch. 1, vv. 11–12).

The Bible makes mention of trees repeatedly to describe the richness of Palestine's landscape, and to illustrate figuratively the Jews' life in war and peace. Trees are part of the people's spiritual understanding of God's creation:

ISAIAH
CH. 44, V. 23
Burst into song, you mountains,
you forests and all your trees …

God also expressly refers to his power to uplift, and to destroy, through a metaphor involving trees:

EZEKIEL
CH. 17, V. 24
All of the trees of the forest will know that
I the Lord bring down the tall tree and make
the low tree grow tall. I dry up the green tree
and make the dry tree flourish
I the Lord have spoken, and I will do it.

Most telling of all is the Psalmist's assessment of humankind, whose nature is compared with the characteristics of trees; humanity's ability to choose to do good things is likened to the palm, and human growth and physical vigour is compared to the cedar:

The righteous will flourish like a palm tree,
they will grow like a cedar of Lebanon;
planted in the house of the Lord,

PSALM
92, vv. 12–15

they will flourish in the courts of our God.
They will still bear fruit in old age,
they will stay fresh and green,
proclaiming, "The Lord is upright;
he is my rock, and there is no wickedness in him."

It can be fairly argued, however, that neither of these trees can claim to be first in the people's hearts and minds. There is an ancient tradition, still practised by people in many countries, of there being a special 'meeting tree' where the village elders gather and where special holy rites are conducted. Examples of such trees can be found in areas as diverse as the Gambia, West Africa, and on the Salt Trail in the foothills of the Himalayas in Nepal.

The association between individual trees and people has a long history, not just in biblical times. In Europe, the Roman writer Pliny the Elder (23–79 AD) wrote that the veneration of trees was a universal custom. In North America giant Californian Redwoods (*Sequioia* species) were venerated (and still are, if the rate at which tourists visit them is anything to go by). There the famous environmental writer, Henry David Thoreau, declared in the mid-1850s (in *Atlantic Monthly*) that people needed forests 'for inspiration and our own true recreation'. In England the association was recorded in Thomas Hardy's novel *The Woodlanders* (published 1887). Now, in the twenty-first century, the Woodland Trust and National Trust are running a project called the Ancient Tree Hunt/Ancient Tree Inventory, to make a database of all of the UK's great and ancient trees. The project was launched in 2004, and by 2020 details of more than 180,000 trees had been uploaded by participants from all walks of life. There are still many more trees waiting to be dealt with. A very high proportion of these ancient trees in the UK are oaks, and individual ancient oaks in the Holy Land are also mentioned in the Bible.

Our examination of specific trees really begins with the wanderings of Abraham and the Israelites (originally he was known as Abram, but was later to be renamed Abraham by God), in the seventeenth century BC after Abraham was told he was to leave his homeland in Mesopotamia and go west to a new land:

The Lord had said to Abram, "Leave your country, your people and your father's household and go to the land I will show you." ... So Abram, left as the Lord had told him ... and they set out for the land of Canaan, and they arrived there. Abram travelled through the land as far as the site of the great tree of Moreh at Shechem ... The Lord appeared to Abram and said, "To your offspring I will give this land." So he built an altar there to the Lord, who had appeared to him.

GENESIS
CH. 12, VV. 1-7

A famous sanctuary already existed at Shechem, which is on the edge of the Plain of Philistia to the west of the Dead Sea. A great tree was often a special feature of such a holy place, so it was a natural place for Abraham to pitch camp. A more telling reason is that clearly Abraham continued to worship his one true God, and it is thought that he camped here so that his own large herds of sheep, cattle and goats did not damage the cultivated land of the Canaanites. We have, then, perhaps the first written reference to a human being showing consideration and thoughtfulness about his relationship with the environment, the study of which we call *ecology*. Abraham's animals could graze under the trees in the wooded foothills. This holy site is also mentioned later in the beginning of Genesis ch. 35:

Then God said to Jacob [Abraham's grandson], "Go up to Bethel and settle there, and build an altar there to God who appeared to you when you were fleeing from your brother Esau."

Jacob does so by the tree at Shechem, which is named as an oak in verse 4. He calls the place El Bethel, which means 'God of Bethel'. The holiness of the site was further emphasized and the tree named when:

GENESIS
CH. 35, V. 8

Deborah, Rebekah's nurse died [Rebekah was the mother of Esau and Jacob] *and was buried under the oak below Bethel. So it was named Allon Bacuth* [which means 'Tree of Weeping'].

There is also 'a great tree' mentioned in 1 Samuel ch. 10 and Judges ch. 9. Only one of the references names the tree as an oak. In modern Israel, there are several species of oak, and unfortunately there are five Hebrew words in the Bible that are indiscriminately translated as 'oak': *'ayl, 'elah, 'elon, 'allah, 'alon*. From Isaiah ch. 6, v. 13 it appears that the *'elah* is different from the *'allon*; in fact, *'ayl, 'elah* and *'elon*, are understood by some to be the terebinth, and *'allah* and *'allon* to represent the oak. The best-known genus of oak trees is *Quercus*. This genus is represented in Palestine by seven species, of which three are common in Palestine.

KERMES OAK

Abraham had a great sensitivity to the sacredness of land and what grows there, and it was not long before he became even more conscious of the dangers of overgrazing, agreeing with his nephew Lot, who had travelled (with his people and herds) with Abraham, that they should separate. Lot chose the plain of Jordan near Sodom, and Abraham went in the opposite direction to the hills of Hebron, and settled among 'the great trees of Mamre' (Genesis ch. 13, v. 18). It is not surprising that Abraham chose the land of the oaks as a place to settle. This was very near the holy site at Shechem. Once again, he prevented what might have been environmental damage and tribal strife by keeping away from existing settlements. He was almost certainly in well-wooded oak habitat.

In Canaan, this part of modern Israel, the most widespread species of oak is the Kermes Oak (*Quercus coccifera*) – those 'great trees of Mamre' may not have been this species, as it is not especially 'great', but there were certainly likely to have been plenty of kermes oaks around. This species is native to the Mediterranean region, and is an evergreen scrub oak, growing up to 5 m (16 ft) tall, but rarely taller than 2 m (6 ft), with stiff, spiny leaves. One nineteenth-century writer, Dr Hooker, wrote, 'It covers the hills of Palestine with a dense brushwood of trees … thickly covered with small evergreen rigid leaves, and bearing acorns copiously.'

This tree is an important food plant for a species of scale insect, *Kermes vermilio*, one of a group of insects from which a crimson-red dye is obtained from the female. The tree's scientific species name reflects this association – *coccifera* means 'carrier of the *coccum* insect' (*coccum* was the Latin name for the insect). The dye, a rich red colour with a hint of violet, was known as early as the eighth century BC. As many as 20,000 insects were needed to produce about 300 g (10 oz) of the dye. The name Canaan actually means 'Land of Purple' because of the importance to the local economy of the dyeing industry. Today, the tree's distribution is much reduced by the spread of the larger (up to 25 m/80 ft tall) Evergreen or Holm Oak (*Quercus ilex*), and by deforestation over the centuries for the production of charcoal and for agricultural ground. Kermes Oak is a hardy tree, able to flourish on rough, hilly ground. Saplings from its acorns grow easily, and it can withstand quite heavy grazing. Abraham settled well. Later the Lord appeared to Abraham near the great trees of Mamre and promised that Sarah, his wife, would have a son, and in due course Isaac was born.

A much less happy tale of an oak is in the story of the death of David's friend, Absalom. David had amassed a Judean army to fight against Israel, in whose army was Absalom. David had appointed three commanders, one of whom was Joab, and instructed them not to harm his friend.

2 SAMUEL
CH. 18, VV. 9-10

*Now Absalom happened to meet David's men.
He was riding his mule, and as the mule went
under the thick branches of a large oak, Absalom's
hair got caught in the tree. He was left hanging in
midair, while the mule he was riding kept on going.
When one of the men saw this, he told Joab,
"I have just seen Absalom hanging in an oak tree."*

Joab angrily told the soldier he should have killed him and received a reward of gold. Despite the soldier's reminding him of David's instruction, Joab took three javelins, and with 10 of his armour bearers, went and killed Absalom, threw him in a big pit in the forest and covered the body with rocks. David's sorrow and the aftermath of the battle are told in detail in verses 18 and 19 of the same chapter.

This was not the end of the story of the oak and its relationship to God and the Israelites. Towards the end of Joshua's life, in the late 1300s BC, he assembled all the tribes of Israel together again at Shechem, and there they witnessed that:

JOSHUA
CH. 24, VV. 24-26

*"We will serve the Lord our God and obey him."
On that day Joshua made a covenant for the people
and there at Shechem he drew up for them decrees
and laws. And Joshua recorded these things in the
Book of the Law of God* [now preserved in the

book Deuteronomy]. *Then he took a large stone
and set it up there under the oak near
the holy place of the Lord.* 〜

That was the seventh memorial that the Israelites had erected to remind them of what the Lord had done for them, through faithful leaders such as Moses and Joshua, even though they had several times forsaken the Lord and worshipped other gods. Seven was considered the number of completeness, so this memorial under the sacred tree at Shechem was especially holy for the Israelites.

During all the Israelites' 40 years of wandering in the desert, led by Moses, and the following years in Canaan led by Joshua, they had carried the tablets of the Ten Commandments in the Ark of the Covenant. When Moses was on Mount Sinai talking to God:

〜 EXODUS
CH. 25, VV. 1-16

*The Lord said to Moses, "Tell the Israelites to
bring me an offering ... offerings of gold,
silver, bronze, coloured yarn and fine linen,
ram skins dyed red and hides of sea-cows,
acacia wood, olive oil, spices for anointing oil
and incense ... Then have them make a chest of
acacia wood ... and poles of acacia wood to insert
on the sides of the chest to carry it. Then put in the
Ark the Testimony* [i.e. the Ten Commandments]
which I will give you. 〜

The poles to support the tent and the surrounding walls, which together made up the travelling, portable Tabernacle (forerunner of the Temple), were also made of acacia, as were the table and the altar inside it. Beyond these furnishings was curtained off the Holy of Holies, where the Ark of the Covenant was kept; only the High Priest was allowed there.

There are hundreds of species of acacia, related to mimosas, across the world, growing in tropical or warm climates. Most of those in the Middle East are not tall trees like the oaks but are hardy, thorny bushes or shrubs just a few metres tall. These bushy-crowned little shrubs are a distinctive feature of semi-desert. Almost certainly, the 'burning bush' from which God spoke to Moses (Exodus, ch. 3, v. 2) was an acacia. Maybe it was the one we now know as the

Negev Acacia

Negev Acacia (*Acacia gerrardii*); this species is common on the Sinai peninsula where Moses had his meeting with God.

As they wandered after they left Egypt, the most common trees the Israelites would have seen would have been these various similar species of acacia. They produce a hard, durable, close-grained wood, which is generally avoided by wood-eating insects, so it makes good furniture. The Red Acacia (*Acacia seyal*) is thought to be the species known in Hebrew as the *shittah-tree*. This tree supplied the *shittim-wood*, as recorded in Exodus ch. 25–30, which the Jews used for the building of the Ark of the Covenant. Emmanuel Swedenborg (1688–1722), the Swedish scientist and theologian, wrote that it 'denotes the good of merit and of justice, which is of the Lord alone'. That is a fitting way to describe the use to which the Israelites put it. Canon Henry Tristram wrote that 'There can be no question as to the identity of the Shittah with the acacia, the only timber tree of any size in the Arabian desert.' It flourishes in the driest situations, scattered over the Sinai peninsula, and in the ravines that open into the Dead Sea.

The Red Acacia is perhaps best known today for its commercial value. It is one of two species of acacia that produce gum arabic. This is used in medicines, the food industry, by artists as a paint thickener, in the production of ceramics and in lithography (the way many of this book's pictures would originally have been printed). The 'burning bush' that Moses saw was most likely an acacia that was brightly back-lit by the sun. The prophet Joel in maybe the ninth century BC passed on a blessing from God to the Israelites:

 JOEL
CH. 3, V. 18

In that day the mountains will drip new wine,
and the hills will flow with milk;
all the ravines of Judah will run with water.
A fountain will flow out of the Lord's house
and will water the valley of acacias.

The acacia is one of several trees mentioned to show how richly fertile the land will become, in this poetic rendering by the prophet Isaiah of words of help and hope from God to the Israelites who were in exile in Babylon in the sixth century BC:

I will turn the desert into pools of water,
and the parched ground into springs.
I will put in the desert

the cedar and the acacia, the myrtle and the olive.
I will set pines in the wasteland,
the fir and the cypress together,
so that people may see and know,
may consider and understand,
that the hand of the lord has done this,
the Holy One of Israel has created it. ⤚

Moses said that the Lord had chosen Bezalel to be chief craftsman in command of the skilled men who were to make the travelling temple, the Tabernacle and the Ark.

Bezalel made the Ark of acacia wood – two and
a half cubits long, a cubit wide, and a cubit and
a half high [that is, about 1.1 m/3¾ ft long x 0.7 m/2¼ ft wide and high].

This Ark was designed to be carried, fixed at the base to two long acacia poles. Interestingly, its design compares closely with a roughly contemporary shrine found in the tomb of King Tutankhamun of Egypt (who died in around 1350 BC). Moses would surely have seen this sort of shrine during his time growing up in Egypt. But the Ark and the supports to the Tabernacle were not the only things made of wood. The furnishings in the Holy of Holies – the table, the altar of incense and the altar of burnt offerings – were also made of acacia.

Apart from the very detailed description of the building of the Ark in Exodus, acacia is mentioned only twice elsewhere; in the retelling of the Ark's construction in Deuteronomy, and in the words of Isaiah above.

Earlier the prophet had described how the wooded landscape changed, firstly deforested by felling, then being restored naturally (ch. 14, vv. 5–8). For centuries the kings of Babylon and Assyria had sent woodsmen to fell and take away cedars, the Lebanon Cedar (*Cedrus libani*) in particular, because they were greatly prized timbers in the construction of buildings. When King Solomon wanted to build a temple, he no doubt remembered that his father King David had built a palace with the help of cedar logs and carpenters sent by King Hiram of Tyre (2 Samuel ch. 5). Hiram remembered too, and:

*When Hiram king of Tyre heard that Solomon
had been anointed king to succeed his father
David, he sent envoys to Solomon ... [and Solomon
replied saying] "Give orders that cedars of
Lebanon be cut for me. My men will work with
yours, and I will pay you for your men whatever
wages you set." ... So Hiram sent word to Solomon:
"I have received the message you sent me and will
do all you want in providing the cedar and pine
logs. My men will haul them down from
Lebanon to the sea, and I will float them
in rafts by sea to the place you specify."*

1 KINGS
CH. 5, vv. 1-9

All this began in the fourth year of Solomon's reign, in about 966 BC, and took about seven years to complete, involving thousands of men, mostly non-Israelite conscripts, organized by Adoniram, who had done the same responsible work for King David. The temple's measurements are carefully recorded in 1 Kings ch. 5 v. 8 and 2 Chronicles ch. 1, v. 7: 60 cubits long, 20 cubits wide and 30 high – that is, about 27 x 9 x 13.5 m (90 x 30 x 45 ft). The temple was roofed with beams and cedar planks; beams of cedar attached side rooms to the building; and the interior walls of the temple were lined from floor to ceiling with cedar boards, so that no stone could be seen. The floor was covered with pine planks, which were most probably from the Mediterranean Cypress (*Cupressus sempervirens*), the third most valuable tree at this time, alongside the oak and the cedar.

Another contender for the wood could be the Aleppo Pine (*Pinus halepensis*), which is native to the whole Mediterranean region. It is a big tree, up to 25 m (82 ft) tall. Isaiah quotes God's promise that He 'will set pines in the wasteland, the fir and the cypress together' (Isaiah ch. 41, v. 19). It is valued for its fine, hard timber. There is doubt among scholars about the translation of the word that becomes 'pine'; 'fir' is more secure, and Canon Henry Tristram in his book says the Aleppo Pine 'is especially the Fir Tree of Scripture, and is only inferior to the Cedar in size'. In English today we still use 'fir' and 'pine' indiscriminately.

Some translations replace 'cypress' with 'box' in Isaiah ch. 41, vv.18–19. The Common Box (*Buxus sempervirens*) would certainly have been familiar to the people of that time. It is an evergreen shrub or small tree, which is native to a broad swathe of Europe and Asia, including around the Mediterranean. It is notoriously slow growing, so that its wood is

Common Box

exceptionally hard, dense and fine grained, making it suitable for use in small, decorative pieces. Box hedging is very popular in Britain – the foliage of small, densely packed leaves lends itself to precise ornamental shaping, whether this be a neatly square-cut hedge, or a more elaborate living sculpture. Sadly, box trees in Europe are now under attack by an invasive species of moth, introduced from eastern Asia. This pretty moth's caterpillars can defoliate box trees and hedges at astonishing speed.

The Holy of Holies was built within the main building, also using much cedar wood, but having the five-sided door jambs and the doors themselves made of wood from another well-known native tree, the Olive (*Olea europaea*). On the walls around the temple, images of palm trees and open flowers were carved, which made the whole place seem like a recreation of the Garden of Eden. Two large cherubims, carved from olive wood and covered with gold, embellished the inner sanctuary, and stood as guardians by the Ark.

ALEPPO PINE

The olive tree is full of beauty, especially when laden with fruit, as the prophet tells us: 'a leafy olive-tree, fair with goodly fruit' (Jeremiah 1, v. 16). It is an evergreen, and the righteous who take refuge in the protection of God are compared to it:

> PSALM   *But I am like an olive tree*
> 52, v. 10   *flourishing in the house of God.*

The wild olive tree grows in the groves of Upper Galilee and Carmel. It is a small, prickly shrub or tree producing small fruits. The olive's foliage is dense and when it becomes old, the fairly tall trunk acquires a unique pattern of repeated rectangles on its bark. The olive is a long-lived species; there are trees in Israel estimated to be 1,000 years old, such as the one in the garden of Gethsemane in Jerusalem. In old age the tree becomes hollow but the trunk continues to grow thicker, at times achieving a circumference of 6 m (20 ft). The most venerable of specimens eventually grow into marvellous, twisted, gnarled trees. The olive tree blossoms at the beginning of summer and its fruit ripens at about the time of the early rains in October. The 'olive shoots' referred to in Psalm 128 are actually the saplings that sprout from its roots and protect the trunk. If the parent tree is cut down, these saplings ensure its continued existence:

> *Your wife will be like a fruitful vine*
> PSALM *within your house;*
> 128, v. 3 *your sons will be like olive saplings*
> *round about your table.*

The expression 'to extend the olive branch' means to reach out to an adversary in a bid to put your quarrels to rest. The olive as a modern symbol of peace is typically depicted as an olive leaf or leafy twig in the bill of a dove. This concept can trace its origin back to the story of Noah's dove, which was sent out in search of dry land after the Ark had been afloat for many days. On her first excursion she returned with nothing, but Noah sent her out again a week later. This time, she returned to the Ark carrying an olive leaf, demonstrating that, somewhere, the waters of God's anger had begun to recede (Genesis ch. 8, v. 11).

Olive wood is very hard and beautifully grained, making it suitable for the manufacture of small articles and ornaments; these shaped and polished pieces are both durable and very attractive. The hollow trunk of the mature tree, however, renders its wood unsuitable for larger objects such as pieces of furniture. Some commentators, therefore, say that the olive cannot be the wood (*ez shemen*) from which the doors of Solomon's Temple were made:

> 1 KINGS *For the entrance of the inner sanctuary he made*
> CH. 6, v. 31 *doors of olive wood with five-sided jambs.*

The entrance to the main hall had similar doors from olive wood, so the scripture says.

Solomon also built a huge Palace of the Forest of Lebanon for himself (1 Kings ch. 7), with four rows of cedar columns supporting 45 cedar roof beams, and much cedar wood panelling from floor to ceiling. Although the scriptures note precisely the number of items in the temple's furnishings, we are not told how much timber was felled and used. The deforestation caused just to complete this project must have been considerable, and appears to go counter to the King's desire to decorate the interior with splendid carvings of God's creation.

Was Solomon's desire to build the best he could imagine for God's house any different from that of the godly men in Europe who built the enormous Christian cathedrals of

Olive

LAUREL

Canterbury, Notre Dame and St Peter's? Even today, people still build huge temples or churches, when this seems to them to be the best way in which they can show their devotion to God. The National Cathedral in Brasilia, Brazil, the extraordinary La Sagrada Familia cathedral in Barcelona and the Crystal Cathedral of glass in Garden Grove, California, USA, are just three spectacular, modern examples.

Time, along with the exploitation of the cedars' wood, has led to a decrease in the number of cedar trees in Lebanon. However, Lebanon is still known for its Lebanese cedars, as they are the emblem of the country and the symbol of the Lebanese flag. The trees survive in mountainous areas, where they are the dominant tree species. This is the case on the slopes of Mount Makmel, which towers over the Kadisha valley, where the 'Cedars of God' are found at an altitude of more than 2,000 m/6,600 ft. Some trees here have reached a height of more than 40 m (115 ft) and their trunks exceed 2.5 m (more than 8 ft) in diameter.

In some translations, the 'green tree' mentioned in Ezekiel ch. 17 v. 24 (see p. 14) is specified to be a 'green laurel tree'. The Laurel or Bay Tree (*Laurus nobilis*) is also mentioned by name in some translations of Psalm 37, although the New International Version does not specify the tree species:

> ⟾ PSALM *I have seen a wicked and ruthless man*
> 37, v. 35 *flourishing like a luxuriant native tree* ⟾

The foliage of the bay tree is indeed luxuriant. It is also fragrant – the addition of just one or two leaves to a stew or sauce imparts a distinctive sweet flavour, although it is not advisable to eat the leaf afterwards. In Ancient Greece, a laurel wreath worn on the head denoted high status and was given to the winner of an athletic contest; in Rome a successful commander was crowned with a laurel wreath. Today, we describe one who has achieved success in the past but has now become lazy to be 'resting on their laurels'. The tree itself is a smallish evergreen, native to the Mediterranean region, but very popular in ornamental gardens both for its lush appearance and as a ready source of seasoning.

In many cultures today people plant a tree as a memorial to a significant event in their lives. So it was in Abraham's life. He moved into the region of the Negev and met Abimelech, King of Gerar, on the edge of Philistine territory. The king tried to take Sarah for his wife, as Abraham had said she was his sister (when in fact she was his own wife). God intervened (the story is worth reading), and eventually the confusion was resolved and a treaty was sworn between them.

So that place was called Beersheba,
because the two men swore an oath there.
After the treaty had been made at Beersheba,
Abimelech and Phicol the commander of his forces
returned to the land of the Philistines. Abraham
planted a tamarisk tree in Beersheba, and there he
called upon the name of the Lord, the Eternal God.

GENESIS
CH. 21, VV. 31-33

The Athel Tamarisk or simply Tamarisk (*Tamarix aphylla*) is a small shrub or tree that can thrive in arid regions. Its rather feathery, leafy branches (*aphylla* means 'without leaves') provide welcome shade, and its dense spikes of pink flowers make it a noticeable feature of the landscape. It was common for leaders to hold official meetings under special trees. Saul had an angry meeting with his commanders under a Tamarisk tree when he learned that David, who had fled Saul's anger, had been discovered (Genesis ch. 22), and after Saul's death in battle, he was buried under a Tamarisk at Jabesh, south of the sea of Galilee (1 Samuel ch. 31).

TAMARISK

The Tamarisk, or at least one of its associations, is recognized today in a popular expression. When someone receives an unexpected gift, which fulfils a need – such as some money or a prize – the recipient or any interested (or envious) onlookers may exclaim 'Manna from heaven!' Many will understand that this is a biblical reference, but may not really know what manna is. The answer is about 3,500 years old. At this time, the Israelites had been captives in Egypt for many years and were at last freed by the Pharaoh. They then miraculously crossed the Red Sea, which drowned the pursuing Egyptian charioteers, and were led by Moses into the bleak and barren desert. Things seemed to be going from bad to worse.

In the desert the whole community
grumbled against Moses and Aaron.
The Israelites said to them, "If only we had
died by the Lord's hand in Egypt.
There we sat around pots of meat and
ate all the food we wanted,
but you have brought us out into this desert
to starve this entire assembly to death."

EXODUS
CH. 16, VV. 2-4

Then the Lord said to Moses, "I will rain down
bread from heaven for you.
The people are to go out each day and gather
enough for that day."

Moses and Aaron told the people this good news and the later promise of God that 'at twilight you will eat meat, and in the morning you will be filled with bread'.

EXODUS

vv. 2-4 AND 13-15

That evening Quail came and covered the camp,
and in the morning there was a layer of dew
around the camp. When the dew was gone,
thin flakes like frost on the ground appeared
on the desert floor. When the Israelites saw it
they said to each other, "What is it?"
For they did not know what it was.
Moses said to them, "It is the bread the
Lord has given you to eat."

Clearly this was not bread as we know it, but it is one of the first times we read in the Bible about a named food. Our word 'manna' comes from the Hebrew words that the Israelites spoke in their grumbling to Moses: *'man hu'*, which simply means 'what is it?'. Our understanding of what it might be has changed over the years. A traditional explanation was that it was a sweet secretion from the Tamarisk tree. More recent study has discovered that this 'manna' is produced not by the tree itself, but by scale insects, which feed on the Tamarisk. Scale insects belong to the 'true bug' order of insects and feed by piercing the stems of plants with their needle-like mouthparts and drinking up the sap. They consume huge amounts of sap to obtain carbohydrates and other trace nutrients, and excrete the excess as 'honeydew'. The white, frosty-looking residue was:

NUMBERS

CH. 11, vv. 7-8

like coriander seed, white, and the taste of
it was like wafers made with honey, and the people
ground it in mills or beat it in mortars, then boiled
it in pots and made cakes of it; and the taste of
it was like the taste of cakes baked with oil.

CITRON

A huge amount of this insect-derived secretion would have been needed to feed the Israelites, which to many readers has seemed ridiculous. We must remember, however, that any attempt at a natural explanation misses the point that the manna and quails in the desert were a miraculous gift from God. That wonderful providence is recalled by Jesus when He called Himself the bread of life. He says to the disciples:

 ST JOHN
CH. 6, VV. 49-51

Your forefathers ate the manna in the desert,
yet they died. But here is the bread which comes
down from heaven, which a man may eat and
not die. I am the living bread that came down
from heaven. If anyone eats of this bread,
he will live for ever.

Most Jewish holidays show a close link between events in their history and the natural, seasonal rhythms of their lives. One such festival, 'The Festival of Booths or Tabernacles' known by them as Sukkot, is still celebrated by the faithful for seven days from the fifteenth day of the seventh month of Tishri (part of our September/October). It is also known as the Festival of the Ingathering; in other words it is a harvest festival, celebrating the bringing in of all the fruit and crops to storehouses. This is one of the Israelites' three Pilgrimage Festivals (with Passover or the Feast of Unleavened Bread to remember the escape from Egypt, and the Festival of Weeks or Harvest to celebrate the first barley harvest). God required his people to collect fruit or foliage from several of the local wild trees as part of the celebration.

God said to Moses:

LEVITICUS
CH. 23, VV. 40-43

On the first day you are to take choice fruit from
the trees, and palm fronds, leafy branches and
poplars [or willows], and rejoice before the Lord
your God for seven days ... All native born
Israelites are to live in booths so that your
descendants will know that I made the Israelites
live in booths when I brought them out of Egypt.

The booth is a temporary shelter. However, even today orthodox Jews in particular will make a booth from willow and palm fronds, decorated with myrtle, and with an offering of fruit, the citron.

The bearer of the 'choice fruit' (Leviticus ch. 23, v. 40), or as the Authorised Version calls it, 'the most majestic fruit', was not specifically named. However, centuries ago the scholars who wrote the commentary on the Hebrew Bible, called the Talmud, declared that the tree in question was the Citron or Etrog (*Citrus medica*), a relative of the lemon, and one of the four original citrus fruits from which all types were developed. Then and now, in the festival it symbolizes hope for fertility and an abundant harvest.

The tree that provided the palm fronds for the Festival of Booths, the Date Palm (*Phoenix dactylifera*) probably originated in the Middle East, but it is now so widely cultivated that its original wild state is unknown. It soon became very important in the lives of the Israelites as they wandered the desert, because palms need water, so where they grow indicates an oasis, a safe place to camp. The people soon learned that the date palm trees not only provided fronds to shelter under and for building, but also high-energy food, camel fodder, and fibres for weaving baskets and rope.

To those who live in the Middle East, the palm tree is probably as important as or more important than the olive. One of the oldest cultivated fruit crops, it has long been harvested for its tasty, fleshy fruit, which is a staple food for many people across North Africa and Arabia. There are many hundreds of varieties of this species, each grown for commercial purposes, perhaps making the date palm the second most familiar palm

DATE PALM

species after the Coconut Palm (*Cocos nucifera*). It grows with an imposing, tall, slender, straight trunk, which has a spiralling pattern on the bark, with long, feather-like leaves that are greenish-grey in colour and have spines on the lower third of the stem. On the upper part of the crown, the leaves stand pointing upwards, but on the lower part, the leaves curve towards the ground. The leaves are rigid, long and pointed, with as many as 200 leaflets growing on each side of the stem. The flowers are clustered into elongated, sheathed inflorescences borne on separate male and female plants. The male's are white and fragrant, and the female's smaller, and more yellowish or cream in colour. The sugar-rich fruit, which is commonly known as the date, is a large, oblong berry that is dark orange when ripe, and may grow up to 7.5 cm (3 in) in length on some cultivated varieties.

2 Chronicles ch. 28, v. 15 records that Jericho is 'the city of palm trees'. Ezekiel chh. 40 & 41 record his vision of a new temple and how a great deal of the structure and carving was with palm wood. But there are only two references to palms in the New Testament. John the Gospel writer describes how in his later great vision he:

 REVELATION
CH. 7, V. 9

looked and there before me was a great
multitude that no-one could count, from
every nation, tribe, people and language,
standing before the throne and in front of the
Lamb. They were wearing white robes and
were holding palm branches in their hands.

But to Christians throughout the world the most memorable reference to palms is at the start of the Easter story:

ST JOHN
CH. 12, VV. 12-14

The next day the great crowd that had come for
the Feast [of the Passover] heard that Jesus was
on his way to Jerusalem. They took palm branches
and went out to meet him, shouting,
"Blessed is he who comes in the name of the Lord!"
"Hosanna!"
"Blessed is the King of Israel!"

All four Gospel writers tell of Jesus's triumphant entry into Jerusalem on what Christians

White Willow

call Palm Sunday, the week before the following Sunday, which is Easter Day. But only John names *palm* branches.

The leafy branches required for the Festival of Booths would probably have come courtesy of willow trees. When the Israelites came to the banks of the River Jordan they found the most abundant plants there were willow trees (*Salix* species), sometimes translated into English as poplars (*Populus* species), and in Hebrew they were *libueh*. The trees in question, which were most likely to have been either the Brook Willow (*Salix acmophylla*) or White Willow (*Salix alba*), or both, are so dependent on a good supply of water that they became a symbol of the Jews' prayer beseeching God to save them from drought by bringing the winter rains, which would enable them to prepare the land for next year's crops. Curiously, another very striking riverside tree of the Holy Land, the Oleander (*Nerium oleander*), is not mentioned in the Bible. Canon Tristram said that this tree 'lines every wadi from Dan to Beersheba, and which beyond every other shrub in the country must rivet the attention of the most unobservant traveller' because of its gorgeous flowers. Was it left out because the Hebrews knew it is poisonous in all its parts and so considered it 'unclean'? Or is it, perhaps, the 'rose bushes in Jericho', or 'a rose growing by a stream of water' (Ecclesiasticus ch. 24, v. 14 and 39, v. 13)? Oleanders have beautiful pink and white blossoms which could give the impression of roses.

The fourth tree which the Jews traditionally brought to the booths was one that the children of Israel found when they reached the Promised Land. Here, they discovered that the hills were covered with forest, and much of it was dense thickets of Common Myrtle, often called simply Myrtle (*Myrtus communis*). Unlike the willows, this tree does not need much water, and sprigs of it will remain fresh for weeks. It is an aromatic plant and may grow more than 5 m (about 16½ ft) high. The opposite leaves are thick and lustrous, with many small, translucent, oil-bearing glands. The solitary white flowers, about 1.8 cm (¾ in) long, are borne on short stalks. The fruit is a purplish-black, a many-seeded berry. Myrtol, a volatile oil found in most parts of the plant, was formerly used as an antiseptic and tonic. In ancient times the myrtle was a symbol of immortality, and so, by extension, a symbol of prosperity and success. The original settlers in the Promised Land clearly felt God was giving them a reminder of this, and the hope for a successful harvest next year.

Perhaps the best-known species of tree in the New Testament is the one commonly referred to as the Sycamore, but it is not the woodland or hedgerow tree familiar to many people in Britain (*Acer pseudoplanatus*). It is more properly translated as the Sycamore-fig (*Ficus sycomorus*). In St Luke's gospel we read the story of Zacchaeus, the tax collector who climbed such a tree (see p. 41). The tree produces good fruit and has been cultivated since at least the third millenium BC. The Ancient Egyptians called it 'The Tree of Life'. The Jews grew it too, but it would appear that one or several were growing wild by the road in Jericho.

After eating from the Tree of Knowledge in the Garden of Eden, Adam and Eve were suddenly aware of their nakedness and sewed fig leaves together to cover their shame. King Sennacherib promised that each Israelite could have his own fig tree. King David appointed Baal-Hanan the Gederite as overseer of his sycamore-figs. Jesus told a parable about a fig tree – its budding showed that the Kingdom of God was close at hand. Zacchaeus, the short-statured tax collector, climbed a sycamore-fig to get a better look at Jesus as He passed through Jericho on His way to Jerusalem.

All of these stories refer to fig trees of the genus *Ficus*, but between them cover two different species – the Common Fig (*Ficus carica*) and the Sycamore-fig (*F. sycomorus*). The fig tree is the first to be given a name that relates to a known species in the Bible, and it is the third of all trees to be mentioned, after the Tree of Life and the Tree of the Knowledge of Good and Evil (Genesis ch. 3, v. 7).

Sycamore-figs are large trees up to 20 m (65 ft) tall, with a dense crown of spreading branches. They are mostly found in Africa south of the Sahara, but long ago were naturalized in Egypt and Israel and grown as an orchard fruit tree. Evidence of the cultivation of sycamore-figs in Old Testament times is told by the prophet Amos when he describes his occupation to Amaziah the priest:

AMOS
CH. 7, V. 14

I was neither a prophet nor a prophet's son,
but I was a shepherd, and I also took care
of Sycamore-fig trees.

A particular sycamore-fig is perhaps the best-known individual tree in the New Testament due to the story of Zacchaeus, found only in St Luke's gospel. These trees' wide canopy is certainly sturdy enough for a grown man to climb high into their branches:

ST LUKE
CH. 19, VV. 1-4

Jesus entered Jericho and was passing through.
A man was there by the name of Zacchaeus;
he was a chief tax collector and was wealthy.
He wanted to see who Jesus was, but being a
short man he could not, because of the crowd.

Oleander

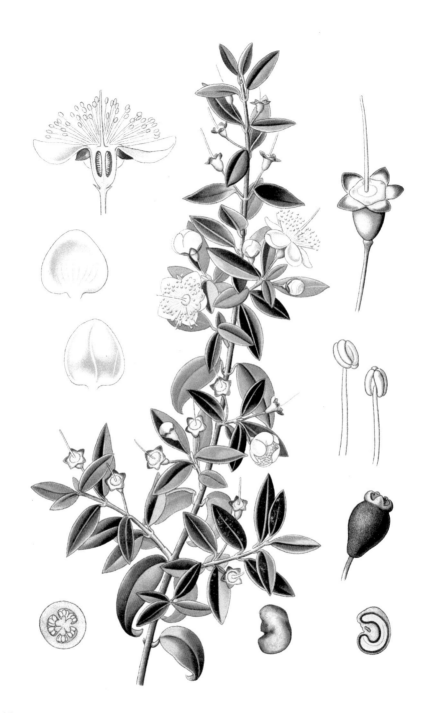

MYRTLE

So he ran ahead and climbed a Sycomore-fig Tree
to see him, since Jesus was coming that way. ≋

He did see Jesus, but more to the point Jesus saw him. Although Luke writes that Jesus was originally just passing through Jericho, He made a point of speaking to Zacchaeus, and inviting Himself to stay at his house. Zacchaeus was thrilled, although the crowd was not: 'He's gone to be the guest of a 'sinner', said some. Tax collectors like Zacchaeus, men in the employ of the Romans for extorting money from the Israelites, were all condemned as far as the faithful were concerned. But Jesus recognized a wonderful opportunity to preach one of His most important messages. Zacchaeus repented of his greed and promised to repay what he had gained by cheating:

≋ ST LUKE

CH. 19, vv. 9-10

Jesus said to him, "Today salvation has come
to this house, because this man, too,
is a son of Abraham. For the Son of man
came to seek and to save what was lost." ≋

Jesus saw that Zacchaeus was a true Jew, even though the crowd did not. Jesus's last sentence quoted above is a splendid summary of His purpose here on earth – to bring salvation to all, which meant eternal life and being part of the kingdom of God.

As already out, the sycamore-fig is quite different from the Sycamore (*Acer pseudoplatanus*), a widespread European species which many people in Britain know well as a common wild tree. The tree in Zacchaeus's story was called just 'sycamore' in the Authorized Version of the Bible. Modern scholarship has corrected later translations.

Common Figs were (and are) cultivated throughout Palestine. A summer tree in full leaf gives cool, welcome shade on a hot day, which is almost certainly why Micah wrote in about 700 BC that:

≋ MICAH

CH. 4, v. 4

Every man will sit under his own vine
and under his own fig tree,
and no-one will make them afraid,
for the Lord Almighty has spoken. ≋

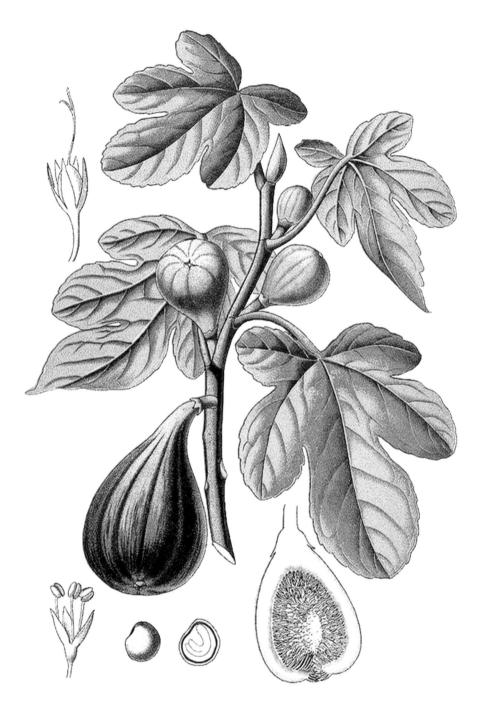

Common Fig

An appreciation for the cool tranquillity afforded by the shady canopy of trees has long been recorded in printed works. In 1825 the American poet William Cullen Bryant published *Forest Hymn*, in which he declared that:

> *The grove's were God's first temples. Ere man learned*
> *To hew the shaft and lay the architrave*
> *And spread the roof above them – ere he framed*
> *The lofty vault, to gather and roll back*
> *The sound of anthems; in the darkling wood*
> *Amidst its cool and silence, he knelt down,*
> *And offered to the Mightiest solemn thanks*
> *And supplication.*

Thus it was in the time of the Patriarchs, and for many believers, so it is still.

CHAPTER 11

FRUITS & OTHER CROPS

Many trees, shrubs and herbaceous plants produce edible fruits (for the purposes of this book, we include nuts within this category). They were and still are a key food source for people living in the Holy Land, and as such have important religious significance. Some of the trees have already been mentioned in the previous chapter, but in this chapter we focus our attention more closely on their fruits, rather than the trees themselves. We also consider the grains, tubers and other edible plant parts that were cultivated or collected in biblical times.

The first individual fruit we encounter in the Bible, the 'apple' that grew on the Tree of Knowledge in the Garden of Eden, was probably actually an apricot, as were 'apples' mentioned later on, for example at various points in *Song of Songs*. The Apricot (*Prunus armeniaca*) is native to Asia but has such a long history of cultivation that its true native range is not known with any certainty. Apricot fruits have golden skin that is smooth to the touch, rather than fuzzy like that of the related peach. They vary in size and flavour but a good apricot has sweet, almost perfumed flesh, surrounding a single seed or stone. No wonder Adam and Eve found it so tempting, and no wonder it is mentioned repeatedly in the sensuous words of *Song of Songs*.

Almonds are also often mentioned in the Bible. The sweet nuts that this tree bears have long been enjoyed by anyone able to break open their hard shells, and are more popular than ever today in the Western world. Ground almonds provide a useful substitute in baking for conventional wheat flour, for those with a gluten allergy or sensitivity, and almond 'milk' (made by soaking almonds in water for a couple of days, then liquidizing them) is an increasingly popular alternative to dairy milk. Almonds' distinctive flavour is the hallmark of many traditional sweet foods enjoyed in Britain, including the marzipan that sits under the icing of our Christmas cakes, and the frangipane topping of a Bakewell tart. Today, the world's largest producer of almonds by far is the United States, but the nuts are also cultivated widely in the Mediterranean region.

The Almond Tree (*Prunus dulcis*) grows up to 10 m (33 ft) tall and begins to bear fruit once it reaches its third year. It is native to Palestine and the Middle East and is often the first tree of the year to put forth blossom, before the leaves appear, as early as January. Carvings

APRICOT

of almond flowers were on the woodwork of the tabernacle, which held the Ark of the Covenant. The pale pink flowers of the almond are possibly the blossoms mentioned in *Song of Songs*, and in *Jeremiah*. The almond tree is revealed to be even more important in the story of the Israelites' anger with Moses and Aaron, and the revolution stirred up by Korah of the tribe of Levi against Moses and Aaron. Moses says God will sort the problem out, and so:

≈ NUMBERS
CH. 17, VV. 1-5 & 8

The Lord said to Moses, "Speak to the Israelites and get twelve staffs from them, one for each of the ancestral tribes. Write the name of each man on his staff. On the staff of Levi write Aaron's name, for there must be one staff for the head of each ancestral tribe. Place them in the Tent of the Meeting in front of the Testimony, where I meet with you. The staff belonging to the man I choose will sprout, and I will rid myself of this constant grumbling against you by the Israelites. … The next day Moses entered the Tent of the Testimony and saw that Aaron's staff, which represented the house of Levi, had not only sprouted but had budded, blossomed and produced almonds. ≈

After this ritual was completed, there was now no uncertainty. The importance of the role of Aaron the priest and his sons in the worship of Israel was firmly grounded.

Clearly, this tree and its fruits have long played a sacred part in Jewish life. It is thought that almond trees were first cultivated in ancient times in the Levant, so Jacob would have been familiar with groves of the trees. On the other hand, the command of Jacob to pack the nuts of the Pistachio (*Pistacia vera*) is the only reference to this tree in the Bible. Pistachios are native to the Middle East, including Israel, and have been cultivated for many centuries. At an archaeological dig in the Hula Valley, in Israel, seeds and nut-cracking tools were found and dated to 78,000 years ago.

PISTACHIO

Soon after the almond trees blossom, the scarlet blooms of the Pomegranate (*Punica granatum*) come out. This tree was cultivated for its much-prized, spherical fruits since ancient times, from Egypt to Mesopotamia. When Moses talked to God and received the Ten Commandments, he was given a detailed description of the design of the priest's robes that Aaron had to wear when he entered the Holy Place:

 EXODUS
CH. 2, vv. 33-35

Make pomegranates of blue, purple and scarlet yarn round the hem of the robe, with gold bells between them. The gold bells and the pomegranates are to alternate round the hem of the robe. Aaron must wear it when he ministers. ≈

The ripe fruit of the pomegranate contains hundreds of seeds, each contained in a pocket called a sarcotesta. The sarcotestas are tightly squashed together within the fruit, making their shapes irregular and polygonal, and each one has a thin, membranous covering containing a tasty reddish pulp, with a single small seed at the centre. Pomegranates, once considered very exotic in Britain, are now in every supermarket, and pomegranate juice and molasses are extremely popular in Middle Eastern cuisines today. In the Middle East, the pomegranate's fruit had long been considered to be a fertility symbol, perhaps because of its abundance of seeds, and its sacred significance became part of the Israelites' beliefs when they made Aaron's robes with their pomegranate-shaped decorations.

Later, scouts sent by Moses to see what the 'Promised Land' looked like, came back with various fruits:

≈ NUMBERS
CH. 13, v. 23

they cut off a branch bearing a single cluster of grapes. Two of them carried it on a pole between them, along with some pomegranates and figs. ≈

Clearly the size of this grape cluster and the variety of other fruits were strong indications of the richness of the land into which God was leading them. Furthermore, pomegranates were listed by God when he said to Moses:

Observe the commands of the Lord your God, walking in His ways, and revering Him. For the

Pomegranate

> DEUTERONOMY
> CH. 8, VV. 6-9

Lord your God is bringing you into a good land –
a land with streams and pools of water, … a land
with wheat and barley, vines and fig trees,
pomegranates, olive oil and honey; a land where
bread will not be scarce and you will lack nothing.

This list is known as the Seven Species, these being the special products of the land of Israel – all of them cultivatable and all of them derived from native plants. Even honey, the only animal product on the list, cannot exist without an abundant and healthy local flora. Pictures of the pomegranate's distinctive fruit appeared on ancient Judaean coins, and decorative silver globes shaped like pomegranates sometimes cover the handles of scrolls of the Torah.

The juice of the fruit became a favourite drink to enjoy in the summer months, as is made clear by the Beloved to her Lover in the Song of Songs:

> SONG OF SONGS
> CH. 8, V. 2

I would lead you
and bring you to my mother's house –
she who has taught me.
I would give you spiced wine to drink,
the nectar of my pomegranates.

The olive oil mentioned in the quotation from Deuteronomy above leads us to consider another of the 'Seven Species', the Olive (*Olea europaea*). We looked at the form and function of this very well-known Mediterranean tree in the previous chapter, and how its wood was used in biblical times (and still is today). Now we turn our attention to its much-loved fruits, and the olive oil that is extracted from them. There are many varieties of cultivated olives, some being suitable for oil, and some that are better eaten whole, in the form of preserved olives. The fruit, which is rich in oil, is first green, but as it matures it becomes black. A plate of preserved olives, perhaps with their pits removed and replaced with a slice of mild red pimento pepper, is a frequent accompaniment to pre-dinner drinks in many European countries. However, the fruit is notoriously divisive – not all people enjoy its strong and very savoury flavour, especially the uninitiated, who may have expected it to taste like the grapes that it somewhat resembles.

Olive trees have always been extensively distributed and very conspicuous in the landscape of the Mediterranean region, and today there are nearly two million farms with olive groves on the European continent alone. They provide a valuable wildlife habitat, home to a wide variety of insects and birdlife, as well as an important source of local income. Production of olive oil has been traced as far back as 2400 BC, in clay documents found near Aleppo in Syria. Today Israel produces only about half of the oil it needs each year, so imports are vital.

King Sennacherib, who besieged Jerusalem in 701 BC, also made use of a description like the one in Deuteronomy when promising the inhabitants of Jerusalem that he would exile them to a country of like fertility:

> *Make peace with me and come out with me.*
> *Then every one of you will eat from his own vine*
> *and fig tree and drink water from his own cistern,*
> *until I come and take you to a land like your own,*
> *a land of grain and new wine, a land of bread*
> *and vineyards, a land of olive trees and honey.*
> *Choose life not death!*

2 KINGS
CH. 18, v. 32

The Israelites did not leave, but Isaiah the prophet told their king, Hezekiah, that eventually, because of their sins, they would be exiled to Babylon – and that did happen, in 586 BC.

The bounty of Israel is frequently described as 'corn, wine and oil' (Deuteronomy ch. 7, v. 13, et al.), that is, grain (wheat and barley), vines and olives, which formed the basis of Israel's economy. When the Israelites conquered the land they found extensive olive plantations (Deuteronomy ch. 6, v. 11). Western Galilee, the territory of Asher (who was Jacob's son), was – and is – especially rich in olives, so much so that Asher will 'bathe his feet in oil' (ch. 33, v. 24). They flourish in mountainous areas too, even among the rocks, thus producing 'oil out of the flinty rock' (Deuteronomy ch. 32, v. 13). Outside the walls of Jerusalem is 'The Mount of Olives' (Zechariah ch. 14, v. 4). It is named in Hebrew, Har ha-Mishhah, 'The Mount of Oil'. The fruit of the olive also develops well in the plain between Mount Hermon and the coast (the Shephelah Lowland), where it grows near sycamore-figs. These crops were so precious that David appointed special overseers to manage the plantations. As far as we know David did not raise taxes; he financed his court by wealth from his extensive land holdings, as well as by commerce, plunder and tribute from

Olive

subjugated kingdoms – so he depended on his orchards being well looked after:

 1 CHRONICLES
CH. 27, V. 28

Baal-Hanan the Gederite was in charge of the
olive and sycamore trees in the western foothills.
Joash was in charge of the supplies of olive oil.

In spring the olive tree is covered with thousands of small whitish flowers, most of which fall off before the fruit forms. Job's 'comforter', Eliphaz the Temanite, uses this image of the tree in spring, to tell Job that if he is not wise:

JOB
CH. 15, V. 33

He will be like a vine stripped of its unripe grapes,
like an olive tree shedding its blossoms.

The fruits are arranged on thin branches in parallel rows like ears of corn (Zechariah ch. 4, v. 12). After it has ripened, the fruit is harvested in two different ways – either by beating the branches with sticks, or by hand picking. The former method is quicker but results in many branches being broken off, with their fruit still attached. The damage that this does diminishes successive harvests. This method, however, was used in biblical times, and the Bible commands that the fruits that remain on the fallen branches are to be a gift to the poor:

When you beat the olives from your trees, do not
go over the branches a second time.
Leave what remains for the alien [immigrants],
the fatherless and the widow.

The same law also told the farmer not to go over the vines again, for the same reason (Deuteronomy ch. 24, vv. 20, 21). The second method was the more usual from about 200 AD onwards, according to the early part of the Talmud. It was termed *masik* ('harvesting olives'), the fingers being drawn down the branches in a milking motion so that the olives fell into the hand. By this method the harvested olives remained whole and undamaged, whereas by the other the olives were often bruised by the beating. The groves produced olives of different varieties and different sizes, and these were destined for different purposes – for oil to be used in cooking and as fuel in lamps, in preserving, and in religious rituals. Despite these differences, the olive was designated as a standard size for many laws, and the expression 'land of olive trees' was interpreted as 'a land whose main standard of measurement is the olive'.

Today we can buy olive oil or virgin olive oil. The latter will have been produced by traditional, mechanical crushing methods, but non-virgin oils will very likely have been chemically treated, to alter the taste, for example. Unrefined or virgin olive oil has a strong and distinctive olive flavour and is more often used raw instead of being heated for cooking. Its taste – for those who enjoy it – makes it a suitable basis for a dressing for salads, or for mixing with a dash of sweet balsamic vinegar to make a tasty dipping oil for a fresh chunk of crusty bread. Virgin olive oil is widely considered to be one of the healthiest types of oil available, being rich in antioxidants, monounsaturated fats and other trace nutrients.

For centuries the olive has been used in cooking, and in religious practices for healing, strength and consecration. Perhaps the best-known example in the Old Testament of the last use is when Samuel, after the death of King Saul, is led by God to anoint the youngest son of Jesse:

 1 SAMUEL
CH. 16, V. 16

So Samuel took the horn of oil and anointed him in the presence of his brothers, and from that day on the Spirit of the Lord came upon David in power.

In the New Testament, the story of an unnamed woman, identified as a 'sinner', at the home of Simon the Pharisee, is particularly well known in the Christian faith. When Jesus visited Simon the Pharisee's home, the host failed to show Jesus any of the three signs of traditional hospitality – a kiss on the cheek as a greeting, water for bathing dusty feet, and oil for the head. However, the woman did anoint Jesus's feet. Jesus says to Simon:

 ST LUKE
CH. 7, VV. 44-46

*I came into your house. You did not give me any water for my feet.
You did not put oil on my head, but she has poured perfume on my eet.*

The oil's everyday use in the kitchen is told in the story from the ninth century BC, of Elisha the prophet and the widow's jar of oil, which also tells of the importance and power of olive oil. Her husband has died and his creditor is coming to take her two boys away, as settlement for his debts. She cries out to Elisha for help, and he tells her to collect as many jars as she can and pour her little bit of oil into all the jars she collects. The oil, miraculously, does not run out, and she fills every one.

2 KINGS
CH. 4, V. 7

She went and told the man of God and he said,
"Go, sell the oil and pay your debts.
You and your sons can live on what is left."

COMMON FIG

Figs are recorded in both the Old and New Testaments and, as discussed in the previous chapter, Bible references relate to both the Common Fig (*Ficus carica*) and the Sycamore-fig (*F. sycomorus*). The fruits of these trees were highly valued as a food source, and failure of the fig harvest – whether by natural or warlike means – would cause great distress:

JEREMIAH
CH. 5, VV. 15-17

"O house of Israel," declares the Lord,
"I am bringing a distant nation against you –
an ancient and enduring nation ...
they will devour your flocks and herds,
devour your vines and fig-trees."

Common Fig trees lose their leaves in winter and by the end of March are in bud again. Tiny figs form at the same time as the leaves appear, grow to about the size of a cherry, then the majority of them are blown by the wind to the ground. These 'green', 'untimely' or 'winter' figs are collected and can be eaten. Some do develop and become 'very good figs, like those that ripen early' (Jeremiah ch. 24, v. 2). They are known by Micah as 'the early figs that I crave' (Micah ch. 7, v. 1). As these are ripening, little buds of the next crop form further up the branches – these are harvested in August.

For people living in areas where Common Figs grow, plucking a fresh, sun-warmed, violet-skinned fig from its branch and eating it there and then is one of the pleasures of summer. Fresh figs are just as delicious if cut in two, grilled lightly and drizzled with honey, and they can also be dried or sugared for preservation. Besides being eaten fresh or dried, figs in biblical times were also pressed into a solid cake (1 Chronicles ch. 12, v. 40) that could be cut with a knife, as was prepared by Abigail for David before he became king (1 Samuel ch. 25, v. 18); or even used medicinally, as was prescribed for King Hezekiah (2 Kings ch. 20, v. 1). Today, figs are enjoyed in various forms. In Britain, fig-roll biscuits are enduringly popular, the preserved figs forming a sticky filling in a casing of sweet pastry. Figs cooked in wine are the basis of many recipes for the 'figgy pudding' mentioned in the carol 'We Wish You a Merry Christmas' – this alcoholic treat was made even more so by being doused in brandy, then set alight before serving. However, traditional figgy pudding, as recorded from fifteenth-century Britain, was much more bread-like than its modern descendant, and did not contain figs. It did include wine, and some other dried fruits, but also various kinds of meat. The combined ingredients were packaged by being packed tightly inside animal intestines, to keep them from spoiling.

Figs are, technically, not fruits at all but enclosed clusters of flowers. They are pollinated by particular species of small wasp, of the family Agaonidae. The female wasp actually enters the unripe fig and collects nectar and pollen from the flowers inside, fertilizing them in the process and allowing their seeds to develop and ripen. The wasp lays her eggs in the fig and the wasp larvae feed on the pollen. When they mature into adult wasps, the new males chew their way to the outside of the fig, and the females escape through this tunnel and seek out a new fig into which to lay their own eggs. This is a simplified summary of the relationship between figs and fig wasps – studies have shown that, while both may benefit from the association, there is an evolutionary 'arms race' constantly going on between the two species, with each adapting to become better at exploiting the other. Some modern fig varieties are seedless and will ripen without the need for pollination – these can therefore be successfully grown in regions where the wasps do not occur.

The other species of fig mentioned in the Bible, the Sycamore-fig, is recorded several times, firstly when David appoints Baal-Hanaan as warden of his orchards, and later when Solomon makes 'cedar as plentiful as sycamore-fig trees in the foothills' (1 Kings ch. 10, v. 27). To get this tree to bear good, ripe fruit is difficult, as it depends on the complex association with its pollinating wasps. In any case its fruits are smaller and less tasty than those of the Common Fig, but they were still an important food for poorer people in biblical times. The obscure Hebrew word to describe Amos's work taking care of the Sycamore-figs is variously translated as 'dresser of', 'tend' or 'took care of', and physical evidence of this work has been found in the tombs of Ancient Egypt where the fruit was cultivated extensively from the start of the third millennium BC.

In another story, the Parable of the Prodigal son, Jesus mentions another fruit. The errant son described in this story had selfishly taken his inheritance and left home for a foreign land and squandered all his money.

ST LUKE
CH. 15, VV. 14-16

After he had spent everything there was a severe famine in the whole country, and he began to be in need. So he went and hired himself out to a citizen of that country, who sent him to his fields to feed pigs. He longed to fill his stomach with the pods that the pigs were eating, but no-one gave him anything.

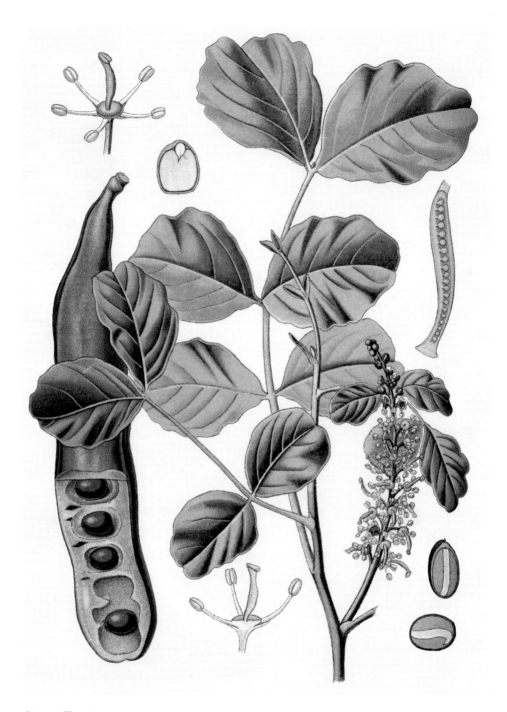

Carob Tree

Once again Jesus preaches a powerful message about the fact that God loves a sinner who repents. The point of His message is made especially sharp by having the boy live with pigs, which to Jews are unclean, so to the Jews listening to Jesus, the boy was a particularly bad sinner.

The pods that the pigs were feeding on were almost certainly the fruits of the Carob Tree (*Ceratonia siliqua*). It is also known as the locust bean and St John's bread. These traditional names may indicate that John the Baptist did not eat honey and locusts in the wilderness, but ate honey and locust beans – a more pleasant prospect, perhaps, although the raw pods and seeds would certainly have been nothing like as delicious as pomegranates or figs. The Carob Tree is a native species of the Middle East and has been cultivated since ancient times. The use of its seed pods during a famine is probably a result of the tree's resilience to the harsh climate and drought. During a famine, the swine were given carob pods so that they would not be a burden on the farmer's limited supplies of more human-friendly foodstuffs. As many will well know, this story has a happy ending. The son is welcomed home by his father, and is forgiven. Indeed, such is the enthusiasm of the welcome that the family's older son, who had stayed at home, is overcome with envy and refuses to attend the festivities, although his father explains to him the special joy of a 'lost' son finally returning to his family.

Today the pod is still important commercially. Locust-bean gum, a powder produced by milling the seeds, is used as a thickening agent in the food industry, and in the production of biscuits and cakes. The pod itself is also dried and milled to produce a sweet powder, which is used as a chocolate substitute. In Malta, carob is used to make *karamelli tal-harrub*, a glassy, crunchy brown sweet that is traditionally eaten during Lent and on Good Friday.

From the first book in the Bible to the last, the Grape (*Vitis vinifera*) is mentioned. Noah, a farmer, was the first person recorded to plant a vineyard, after he, his family and his Ark full of paired animals came on land again after the flood (Genesis ch. 9, vv. 20–23). He also became the first person to drink too much wine and become drunk. Following this over-indulgence, he was discovered naked and insensible by his son Ham. On seeing his father's nakedness, Ham told his two younger brothers, Shem and Japheth. These two covered Noah's nakedness, but were careful to avert their gaze from him. When he recovered, Noah prayed that God would bless these two respectful sons and make them prosper, but placed a curse on Ham, or rather on Ham's son Canaan, as a punishment for having been seen in this state. Why poor Canaan had to bear this burden on his father's behalf is the subject of much debate. It was not unusual in biblical times for children to be punished for a parent's misdeed. However, some scholars believe that it was actually the young boy Canaan who found Noah in his inebriated state and, highly amused by what he saw, called his father over to have a look. In any case, Noah may have been the first biblical figure to drink too much wine, but he was far from the last.

A later writer emphasized wine's power when he wrote 'Don't let wine tempt you, even

though it is rich red' (Proverbs ch. 23, v. 21). Another Old Testament book has an erotic image spoken by a male lover to his beloved, which names our fruit and its tempting power:

SONG OF SONGS
CH. 7, VV. 6-9

How beautiful you are and how pleasing,
O love, with your delights!
Your stature is like that of the palm,
and your breasts like clusters of fruit.
I said, "I will climb the palm tree;
I will take hold of its fruit."
May your breasts be like clusters of the vine,
the fragrance of your breath like apples,
and your mouth like the best wine.

St John, writing in Revelation, the last book, sees a vision of the final judgement of the people of the world. One angel gathers all the righteous people, and another is told to harvest the rest and prepare them to meet their fate:

REVELATION
CH. 14, VV. 18-20

"Take your sharp sickle and gather the clusters
of grapes from the earth's vine, because the grapes
are ripe." The angel swung his sickle on the earth,
gathered its grapes and threw them into the great
winepress of God's wrath. They were trampled in
the winepress outside the city, and blood flowed
out of the press ...

Whatever may be our understanding of this apocalyptic and rather graphic description of the end of the world and the disposal of the world's sinners, it does tell us how the farmers of that time extracted the juice of the grapes. The winepress was a rock-hewn trough about 2.5 m (8 ft) square with a channel on one side leading to a smaller trough. Grapes were thrown in the upper trough and trampled with bare feet, and the juice flowed into the lower trough, to be collected and turned into wine.

The Old Testament has dozens of references to grapes and vineyards and wine, which shows how important the fruit was at that time. But wine was not just for a drink – it was also to be part of the regular sacrificial offerings as recorded in Exodus ch. 29, Leviticus chh. 1–7 and Numbers ch. 28. But above all it is the Psalmist who sums up the Jews' feelings about the vine, the grape and the '*wine that gladdens the heart of man*' (Psalm 104, v. 14).

So, to the Jews the vineyard and what grew there was much more than just a source of sweet food to gladden his heart. The prophet Isaiah (749–681 BC) put it like this in a section of his prophecy often titled as *The Song of the Vineyard*:

I will sing for the one I love
a song about his vineyard:
My loved one had a vineyard
on a fertile hillside.
He dug it up and cleared it of stones
and planted it with the choicest vines.
He built a watchtower in it

≫ ISAIAH
CH. 5, VV. 1-2 & 7

and cut out a winepress as well.
Then he looked for a crop of good grapes
but it yielded only bad fruit ...
The vineyard of the Lord Almighty
is the house of Israel;
and the men of Judah
are the garden of his delight.
And he looked for justice, but saw bloodshed;
for righteousness, but heard cries of distress. ≫

Isaiah describes a special vineyard, then interprets it with a powerful play on words in the last two lines – in Hebrew the words for 'justice' and 'bloodshed' sound alike, as do 'righteousness' and 'distress'. There follows Isaiah's declaration of God's judgement on the sinful nation of Judah which will come, including the fact that 'a ten-acre vineyard will produce only a bath of wine' (about 36 litres/8 gallons), (Isaiah ch. 5, v. 10), which is a very small fraction of what the harvest should be. The total depends on the quality of the grapes, the quality of the land, the density of the planting and careful husbandry; then good wine can be produced from 4–8 tons of grapes *per acre*, and that can give about 700 litres (150–160 gallons) of wine *per ton per acre*. This shows that God's punishment is a really harsh one. Jews today may believe that God's vineyard of Israel is the conquering one now, not the conquered nation Isaiah was describing, but it is certainly not peaceful.

Jesus was also adept at creating telling images from everyday life. One of His most memorable is His Parable of the Tenants of a Vineyard, which is found in Matthew, Mark and Luke. This tale is probably based on Isaiah's *The Song of the Vineyard*. St Matthew tells the parable in detail. A man purchased a vineyard, then travelled abroad and let out the land to tenants. The tenants of the vineyard were greedy and thought they could make it their own, stealing the land from its rightful owner. They killed a servant who the owner had sent to collect some fruit, then beat and stoned another, and a third. Hearing of this, the owner sent his son, who surely would be respected. But the tenants killed him as well, thinking this was the last obstacle standing between them and their successful stealing of the vineyard. Jesus ended the story by asking His disciples what the owner of the vineyard would do next – and the answer was that he would destroy those responsible, and give the vineyard to other, more worthy tenants. The symbolism in the tale – the owner as God, his son as Jesus, and the tenants as Israel's priests and scribes of the time – is widely acknowledged.

This parable was told by Jesus in Jerusalem a little while after He had angrily overturned the tables of the money-changers in the temple. It is one of His statements at this time warning the disciples of His imminent death. For Christians, this parable is a constant reminder that Jesus Christ does indeed hold the Church together. John sums up much of what Christians believe, when he records these words of Jesus:

≫ ST JOHN
CH. 15, VV. 1-3 & 16

I am the true vine, and my Father is the gardener.
He cuts off every branch in me that bears
no fruit, while every branch that does bear fruit
he prunes so that it will be even more fruitful.
You are already clean [that is, pruned] *because*
of the word I have spoken to you. Remain in me,
and I will remain in you. No branch can bear
fruit by itself; it must remain in the vine.
Neither can you bear fruit unless you remain
in me … I chose you and appointed you to go
and bear fruit – fruit that will last. ≫

The disciples and people today still puzzle over what is meant by 'fruit'. Some think it just means that you have persuaded someone to be a Christian. However, a different interpretation is offered by St Paul:

GRAPE

GALATIANS
CH. 5, vv. 16, 22, 23

So I say, live by the Spirit, and you will not gratify the desires of sinful nature ... But the fruit of the Spirit is love, joy, peace, patience, kindness, goodness, faithfulness, gentleness and self-control. Against such things there is no law.

That is a rich harvest of fruit indeed, nine grapes or virtues in one cluster, giving wine of the best quality. These qualities can be seen as the harvest that will enrich the Christians' lives and the Church's evangelism, and ensure all believers will love their neighbours as themselves.

The beginning of the story of the Jews is either lost in myth and legend or, depending on your point of view, recorded carefully in the first book of the Bible, Genesis. After the story of the Creation, the Bible records that the story of the Jews begins with farmers. Today, agriculture in Israel is led by modern technologies, and she exports a considerable amount of fresh produce, despite the fact that about half the country is desert, and that due to the climate there is a shortage of water. The Bible tells us how the tradition of agriculture in the Holy Land first began. The first word in the Hebrew text is *hereshith* ('in [the] beginning'). This is the Hebrew title of the book (our name comes from the Greek Septuagint translation), so it tells of the early history of the Hebrew world. After the stories of the Creation and the Garden of Eden we come to a family tale: the birth of two sons – Cain and Abel – to Adam and Eve.

GENESIS
CH. 4, vv. 1 & 2

Adam lay with his wife Eve, and she became pregnant and gave birth to Cain. She said, "With the help of the Lord I have brought forth a man." Later she gave birth to his brother Abel. Now Abel kept flocks, and Cain worked the soil.

Eventually, each son brings an offering to the Lord of what they have produced. Cain brought 'some fruits' but Abel brought 'fat portions from some of the first born of his flock'. God looked favourably on Abel's generous offering but not so on Cain's casual gift. Cain was jealous that his brother was praised by God, and killed him. When God asked where his brother was, Cain gave a reply that has entered the English language as a saying from someone who claims to have no interest in or responsibility towards the welfare of a sibling or acquaintance: 'Am I my brother's keeper?' (v. 9). When the murder was discovered, Cain's lands were cursed and he was no longer able to grow crops. Instead he had to live out his days as an exiled wanderer (although some of his descendants did rather better for themselves). Sadly, this callous indifference to others is still widespread in the world today, and may result in individuals and nations being like Cain – outcasts.

Archaeological research has revealed that during the early history of the region the people did indeed keep flocks and grow crops. Abraham, Isaac and Jacob were such people; pastoral farmers, semi-nomadic, wandering to find food for their animals. On the other hand, the people of Egypt, thanks to the fertile soil along the Nile valley, led a more settled life and were famous for their bountiful crops of grain. By Christ's time, when the Romans ruled the world, Egypt was 'the bread basket' of the known world. Over the course of centuries, growing crops became increasingly important. At many points in the Old Testament, you will find the listing together of grain, wine, oil and pulses, which shows that these products were the principal harvests of the Palestinian farmer, and the Jews' social and religious year revolved around the several harvest periods (see pp. 33–34).

In 1908 archaeologists digging at the ancient city of Gezer, west of Jerusalem, found an inscribed limestone tablet, which has become known as the Gezer Calendar:

two months gathering [olives] *(September, October)*
two months planting (November, December)
two months late sowing (January, February)
one month cutting flax (March)
one month reaping barley (April)
one month reaping and measuring grain (May)
two months pruning [vines] *(June, July)*
one month summer fruit (August)

Whether these are the words of a popular song or a schoolboy's memory exercise does not really matter – in either case, what they do is clearly reveal the fact that the Palestinian farmer would have been toiling throughout the year. Besides the tasks listed he also had to clear the stony land ready to plough, then had to irrigate the land during the dry season, as is recorded in *The Apochrypha*, by bringing:

 ECCLESIASTICUS   *a brook from a river and …*
        CH. 24, VV. 30-31   *a water channel into a garden*

The descendants of Cain grew two kinds of grain – barley and wheat. The first reference to barley is in the recording of the dreadful catastrophes that overtook Egypt because the Pharaoh refused to let the Israelites leave the country. God told Moses to tell the Pharaoh:

EXODUS

CH. 9, VV. 18 & 31-32

"… at this time tomorrow I will send the worst hailstorm that has ever fallen on Egypt, from the day it was founded till now."
(The flax and barley were destroyed, since the barley was in the ear and the flax was in bloom. The wheat and spelt however, [see p. 74] were not destroyed, because they ripen later.)

We will consider the two cereal grains in the order they are mentioned, which is not the same as their importance or value, as will be seen. Barley (*Hordeum vulgare*) is a cereal grain, a self-pollinating member of the grass family. Its seed heads have a distinctive 'long-haired' appearance due to their elongated awns, or spikes – a field of ripe barley on a breezy day is a beautiful sight to behold. Its wild ancestor grew abundantly in the Fertile Crescent of western Asia, a horseshoe shape of land from Mesopotamia to Upper Egypt. This is the very land of Cain and the Patriarchs of old, so it is perfectly natural that we should find that one of God's laws for them says:

LEVITICUS

CH. 27, V. 16

If a man dedicates to the Lord part of his family land, its value is to be set according to the amount of seed required for it – fifty shekels of silver to a homer [6 bushels or about 220 litres] of barley seed.

In ancient times the shekel was simply a unit of weight of about 11 g (⅓ oz), and it is thought that it originally referred to the weight of barley. Later it became a coin's name as well, and today in Israel it refers only to that country's currency.

Barley was harvested in April or May, depending on the weather and the farm's position. The size of the barley harvest in about 950 BC can be judged from words that King Solomon sent to King Hiram of Tyre as part of his request for wood and workers to help build his new temple:

2 CHRONICLES
CH. 2, VV. 8-10

My men shall work with yours to provide me with plenty of timber, because the temple I build must be large and magnificent. I will give your servants, the woodsmen who cut the timber, 20,000 cors [c. 4,400 kilolitres/120,000 bushels] of ground wheat, 20,000 cors of barley, 20,000 baths [c. 440 kilolitres/95,000 gallons] of wine and 20,000 baths of olive oil.

Hiram agreed to supply the timber, appointed a skilled craftsman to work with Solomon's men, and sent the timber. The quantity of food and drink that Solomon promised was much needed – the end of Chapter 2 records that he ordered 153,000 men to be the work force. By New Testament times it is recorded that a worker gets 'three quarts (about a litre) of barley for a day's wage' (Revelation ch. 6, v. 6).

Barley grains are a nutritious food, rich in protein. Although barley was considered an inferior grain to wheat, its wholemeal flour was and is much used in cooking. Barley today is cultivated in temperate climates around the world, with Russia being the biggest producer. It is the fourth most widely grown grain species by weight, behind maize, rice and wheat. As well as being used to produce flour for baking, the whole grains can be eaten after boiling – hulled and polished 'pearl barley' grains are often added to soups. Barley is also an important crop for animal feed, and is essential in beer and whisky production.

BARLEY

Barley bread is mentioned several times in the Bible. After the death of Joshua, Israel fell into the hands of the Midianites. Their home territory flanked the eastern arm of the Red Sea. It was where Moses fled after he had killed the Egyptian (Exodus ch. 2). After nine years of oppression, Gideon was leader of the desire to be rid of the Midianites:

Now the camp of Midian lay below him in the valley. During the night the Lord said to Gideon, "Get up, go down against the camp, because I am going to give it into your hands. If you are afraid to attack, go down to the camp with your servant Purah and listen to what they are saying ..." Gideon arrived just as a man was telling his friend his dream. "I had a dream," he was saying. "A round loaf of barley bread came tumbling into the Midianite camp. It struck the tent with such force that the tent overturned and collapsed." His friend responded, "This can be nothing other than the sword of Gideon son of Joash, the Israelite. God has given the Midianites into his hands."

⌒ JUDGES
CH. 7, VV. 8-14

Indeed He had. With only 300 men, Gideon routed the enemy, who fled. Revelations by dreams are often mentioned in the Old Testament. This dream's imagery is particularly apposite because the barley of the loaf is worth only half as much as wheat. In this way, it could be interpreted as symbolic for Israel, whose numbers were far fewer than those of the enemy. Gideon would have found much comfort in what he overheard.

In contrast, a splendid, peaceful story that includes the barley loaf is found in all four Gospels, although only St John names what sort of bread is involved. A large crowd has followed Jesus up a mountain. Jesus asks his disciples to solve the riddle of how all of these people are to be fed:

Jesus went up on a mountain and sat down with his disciples. The Jewish Passover feast was near. When Jesus looked up and saw a great crowd coming towards him, he said to Philip,

"Where shall we find bread for these people to eat?"
He asked this only to test him, for he already
had in mind what he was going to do.
Philip answered him, "Eight months' wages would
not buy enough bread for each one to have a bite!"
Another of the disciples, Andrew, Simon Peter's
brother, spoke up. "Here is a boy with five
barley loaves and two small fish, but how
far will they go among so many?"
Jesus said, "Make the people sit down."
There was plenty of grass in that place,
and the men sat down, about five thousand of
them. Jesus then took the loaves, gave thanks,
and distributed to those who were seated as much
as they wanted. He did the same with the fish.
When they had all had enough to eat,
he said to the disciples, "Gather the pieces
that are left over. Let nothing be wasted."
So they gathered them and filled twelve
baskets with the pieces of the five barley
loaves left over by those who had eaten.

≈ ST JOHN
CH. 6, VV. 7-13

Barley loaves were cheap – the food of the poor. The miraculous feeding of the crowd – 5,000 men (and, according to Matthew, an unspecified number of women and children were present too, although it is not clear whether they were also permitted to eat) – was a splendid preface to the meeting later that Jesus had with his disciples when he told them that:

≈ ST JOHN
CH. 6, VV. 26, 34-35

"you ate the loaves and had your fill. Do not work
for food that spoils, but for food that endures to
eternal life, which the Son of man will give you ..."
"Sir," they said, "from now on give us this bread."
Then Jesus declared, "I am the bread of life.
He who comes to me will never go hungry,
and he who believes in me will never be thirsty."

Wheat (Common, Durum, Emmer And English)

This declaration by Jesus is the first of seven I AM descriptions by Jesus of Himself, all recorded only in St John's gospel. The crowd and the disciples did not understand it. They still thought Jesus was talking about real bread. With 'I am the bread' Jesus is echoing God's words telling Moses His name, 'I AM WHO I AM' (Exodus ch. 3, v. 14), and in so saying Jesus is stating His own divinity and putting Himself on a collision course with the authorities; He left the crowd grumbling and arguing, 'How can this man give us his flesh to eat?' The disciples said it was a hard lesson, but Simon Peter finally admitted on their behalf, 'You have the words of eternal life. We believe and know that you are the Holy One of God.' (St John ch. 6, vv. 68, 69). The Christian today finds this is still a hard lesson to understand, and he or she needs the faith of Peter to be able to say 'I believe'.

One of the best-known stories in the Old Testament is the story of Jacob's young son, Joseph. Jacob was father to 13 children, 12 of them boys, and Joseph was the second-youngest boy. The first 11 children were born to Jacob's first wife, Leah, while Joseph and his younger brother Benjamin were the children of Jacob's second wife and Leah's sister, Rachel. Thanks to Andrew Lloyd Webber's musical *Joseph and the Technicolour Dreamcoat*, thousands of people, young and old, know something of the story of Joseph and his family, which is a big feature of the Bible's first book, Genesis. The story begins when:

GENESIS
CH. 37, VV. 2-8

Joseph, a young man of seventeen was tending the flocks with his brothers … Now Israel [that is, Jacob, his father] *loved Joseph more than any of his other sons because he had been born to him in his old age; and he made a richly ornamented robe for him. When his brothers saw their father loved him more than any of them, they hated him and could not speak a kind word to him.*
Joseph had a dream, and when he told it to his brothers, they hated him all the more. He said to them, "Listen to this dream I had: we were binding sheaves of corn out in the fields when suddenly my sheaf rose and stood upright, while your sheaves gathered round mine and bowed down to it."

His brothers, in no doubt as to what the dream seemed to represent, said to him, 'Do you intend to reign over us?' As a result of their jealousy they plotted to kill him, but instead, when they were all out tending their flocks, they sold him to Midianite traders who were on their way to Egypt. That at last brings us firmly to the resolution of the very important story about Joseph's dream about sheaves of corn. In Egypt, Joseph interpreted dreams for servants and the Pharaoh, and was rewarded by the Pharaoh, who put him in charge of all Egypt, which meant that he controlled the saving of the wheat harvest throughout the country:

 GENESIS
CH. 41, V. 49

Joseph stored up huge quantities of grain, like the sand of the sea. It was so much he stopped keeping records because it was beyond measure.

The rest of the family story and its happy ending is told in Genesis chh. 42–47.

Joseph's dream 'corn' is really wheat; in English the word 'corn' has for centuries referred to any form of grain, but nowadays the word technically should refer to maize (*Zea*), a genus of cereals from the Americas, which are now cultivated widely around the world. Wild *emmer* and *einkorn* forms of wheat (*Triticum* species) were first cultivated in the Fertile Crescent. Archaeological evidence of *einkorn* wheat has been discovered in Jordan dating back to 7500–7300 BC, and there is evidence for *emmer* wheat in Iran as old as 9600 BC. The genetics of wheat are complicated. It is self-pollinating and cultivation has resulted in the creation of about 30,000 distinct domestic forms from 14 original species. Today, wheat fields cover more land area than any other type of crop, with varieties of Common Wheat (*Triticum aestivum*) the most widely planted by far. Durum Wheat (*T. durum*) is the second most popular species – its hard grains are used to make flour for pasta.

Many modern wheat strains bear little resemblance to their wild ancestors. Through selective breeding their genetics have been tweaked to increase the size of their grains and change their balance of nutrient content, make the rachis (which attaches the grains to the stem) more robust so that the ears of wheat are less likely to fall apart pre-harvest, make them more resistant to pests and disease, and modify their growth season so that sowing and harvest times can be arranged with more convenience.

In Joseph's time, wheat was harvested in early summer, about a month after barley. Harvesting was labour intensive. The farmer would grasp a handful of stalks in his left hand, cut them fairly high up with a sickle held in the right hand, and bind them into sheaves. Some plants were left growing in difficult-to-reap corners of the field; that and seed fallen to the ground was left for the gleaners, as is told in the story of Ruth. She was a Moabite woman living more than 3,000 years ago, who asked her widowed Israelite mother-in-law if she could go in the fields and pick up the leftover grain. The rest of the story is an intimate, delightful glimpse into family life (Ruth chh. 1–4).

After harvesting and binding the wheat, the farmer still had many other tasks to do. Sheaves were taken to a threshing floor in carts or on the backs of asses. This floor was a circular patch of hard, dry, flat ground, which was usually the common property of the village. A common method of threshing was to scatter the sheaves and drive a hard wood sledge pulled by an ox or two over them. The grain was now freed from the husk but was mixed with broken straw and chaff. This was thrown into the air from a shovel – a process called winnowing – whereupon the heavier grain fell and the chaff blew away. Very often a final cleaning was achieved by sieving the grain. Several times the prophet Isaiah uses images of wheat farming to illustrate what is happening to the Jews, especially when he tells them this message from God:

ISAIAH
CH. 28, VV. 23-29

Listen and hear my voice;
pay attention and hear what I say.
When a farmer ploughs for planting,
does he plough continually?
Does he keep on breaking up and
harrowing the soil?
When he has levelled the surface.
Does he not sow caraway and scatter cummin?
Does he not sow wheat in its place,
barley in its plot, and spelt in its fields?
His God instructs him
and teaches him the right way.
Caraway is not threshed with a sledge,
nor is a cartwheel rolled over cummin;
caraway is beaten with a rod, and cummin with a stick.
Grain must be ground to make bread;
so one does not go on threshing it for ever.

Spelt (*Triticum spelta*) is another form of ancient wheat. It is one of the ancient grains that has found a resurgence of popularity today, with spelt bread being on offer in many an expensive artisanal bakery in Western countries. There is scientific evidence that spelt originated as a hybrid of *emmer* and a wild grass that grew in the Middle East long before common wheat as we know it appeared. Despite the Bible reference, some commentators do not believe spelt was cultivated in Mesopotamia, but is the result of the confusion with *emmer* wheat. Isaiah's poetic parable is thought to be saying that although God must punish Israel, his actions will be as well controlled as a good farmer's would be.

Once the grains were collected, finally the precious crop was stored. If done carefully, it would keep for several years, as Joseph found in Egypt. Underground, bottle-shaped silos were dug, or the grain was kept in big earthenware jars. Modern excavations at Jericho have found millet, barley and lentils in round clay bins, which had been stored more than 5,000 years ago. The joy of the farmer is expressed by the excited words of the Psalmist in a prayer to God:

PSALM
65, vv. 9-13

You care for the land and water it;
you enrich it abundantly.
The streams of God are filled with water
to provide the people with corn,
for so you have ordained it.
You drench its furrows
and level its ridges;
you soften it with showers and bless its crops.
You crown the year with your bounty,
and your carts overflow with abundance.
The grasslands of the desert overflow;
the hills are clothed with gladness.
The meadows are covered with flocks
and the valleys are mantled with corn;
they shout for joy and sing.

Today the harvest is still a time celebrated by people of many faiths. Christians, in both country and city churches, sing harvest songs, such as 'We plough the fields and scatter/The good seed on the land'. City churchgoers sing it even though very few people living in the city have ever ploughed a field or harvested the ripe grain. The believers are mindful of the debt they owe to God for the bountiful food that *is* provided. It may well have come from the supermarket, but someone at home or abroad has put in the hard labour of producing it, helped or hindered by the natural vagaries of weather and climate.

Isaiah's message from God quoted above mentions other crops apart from grain. Vegetables and herbs of various kinds were a part of the everyday diet, but a vegetable garden as we know it was likely to be planted only at the homes of the wealthy. Not withstanding that, the Israelites when they were in Egypt were familiar with several such foods and angrily remarked to Moses early in their escape from the Pharaoh:

WATERMELON

NUMBERS
CH. 11, vv. 4-5

If only we had meat to eat! We remember the fish we ate in Egypt at no cost – also the cucumbers, melons, leeks, onions and garlic.

Many years later Isaiah tells the sinful Israelites that the desolation they have suffered from invaders over at least two centuries has resulted in Jerusalem being no more defensible than a

ISAIAH
CH. 1, v. 8

shelter in a vineyard, like a hut in a field of melons, like a city under siege.

The owner of a vineyard often built a tower there and employed a watch-keeper to protect his crop. The word for 'melons' here is translated as 'cucumbers' in some versions of the Bible. However, the Watermelon (*Citrullus lanatus*) was once common in ancient times in Egypt, where its fruits were a valuable source of water in times of drought. It is now grown widely in Palestine and marketed throughout the land. Worldwide, most of the watermelons grown today are cultivated in China, but the market for these large, sweet, red-fleshed fruits is global. The plant itself is an annual and develops fast-growing, long, trailing stems that produce male and female flowers, the latter developing into the fruits, which are technically oversized berries, after pollination.

The Cucumber (*Cucumis sativus*) has a long history of cultivation. It is native to southern Asia but was brought further west by the Greeks and Romans. However, the other produce mentioned in Numbers ch. 11, vv. 4–5 – leeks, onions and garlic – may all have been found growing wild, as well as in cultivation, in parts of the Holy Land in biblical times. All three are members of the genus *Allium*, and produce attractive clusters of flowers atop a single tall stem – several are grown as ornamental flowers. The Wild Leek (*Allium ambpelopresum*) has been developed into several variants – in the case of the vegetable we

CUCUMBER

Wild Leek

GARLIC

know today as the leek, it is the bundle of leaf sheaths that is cooked and eaten, but in another variant, elephant garlic, the bulb is eaten. Leeks are easy to grow and cook, so would have been a popular addition to a wealthy family's vegetable garden in biblical times.

The Onion (*Allium cepa*) has been cultivated worldwide for many years, perhaps as long ago as 5000 BC, and today is a cornerstone of many different cuisines. However, its wild ancestor is extinct and its historical distribution is uncertain. Garlic (*A. sativum*) is native to central and parts of western Asia. Its pungent bulb adds an unmistakable flavour to all kinds of cuisines around the world, and it is also prized for its medicinal properties – it has an antibacterial effect and has historically been recommended as a treatment for a wide range of health problems.

When Ahab was king of Israel, the northern kingdom, in 874–853 BC, he said to Naboth in Samaria, 'Let me have your vineyard to use for a vegetable garden'. Naboth refused, but Ahab's wife Jezebel plotted against Naboth, had him stoned to death for reportedly having cursed God and the king, and so gained the vineyard. But both Ahab and Jezebel were condemned and eventually executed for these actions (1 Kings ch. 21).

At the end of His life, when Jesus came finally to Jerusalem, He taught the crowds and harangued the hypocrisy of the Saducees and Pharisees, using a homely image to make His point:

ST MATTHEW
CH. 2, V. 23
(ALSO ST LUKE CH. 11, V. 42)

Woe to you, teachers of the law and Pharisees, you hypocrites! You give a tenth of your spices – mint, dill, and cummin. But you have neglected the more important matters of the law – justice, mercy and faithfulness. You should have practised the latter, without neglecting the former.

Jesus does not criticize citizens for observing the law, but rather the hypocrisy of following some parts and not others. Of course, some believers sometimes do just that today, following the liturgy of their favourite church service but failing to love their neighbours as themselves.

These words from Jesus clearly show that vegetables and spices were an important part of life. They were all used to season food. Mints (*Mentha* species) are attractive aromatic perennial plants, with many forms worldwide, including Peppermint (*M. piperita*) and Spearmint (*M. spicata*), which are the two species most widely used in the temperate world in cooking. The leaf is used, fresh or dried, in Europe and the Middle East with lamb, or to

Spearmint

make mint tea. Mint as a flavouring for sweet things is also widely used – 'mints' are mint-flavoured sugary sweets, and mint is often paired with chocolate in ice-cream desserts. The pleasant freshness of its taste makes it the standard flavouring for toothpastes and mouthwashes.

Dill (*Anethum graveolens*) is related to celery. Its leaves are aromatic and are widely used in Europe, the Middle East and Asia to flavour fish, pickles and soup. It is an annual herb. Cumin (*Cuminum cyminum*) is an annual plant in the parsley family, and the seasoning is obtained from the seeds, used dried and ground, or crushed. They provide an earthy, spicy flavour that is the cornerstone of all kinds of highly aromatic curried dishes today. Cumin was a feature of Ancient Egyptian cooking and later part of Jewish, Greek and Roman cuisines, as well as featuring heavily in more easterly nations.

The miraculous manna that feeds the Israelites in Exodus ch. 16 is compared to the seed of Coriander (*Coriandrum sativum*). This annual, herbaceous plant, known in America as cilantro, is a relative of parsley, and its seeds are, like cumin, a popular spice in Indian cuisine today. It is native to southern Europe, northern Africa and southwestern Asia, so would have been well known in biblical times. Its round seeds can be toasted and ground to produce a fragrant powder, but it is the leaves that are more familiar to us today. They have a distinctive taste that many enjoy, but to a minority of people they test soapy and extremely unpleasant. Studies have shown that variations in just one or two genes determine whether the taste of coriander is perceived as pleasant or appalling.

White Mustard (*Sinapis alba*) is another annual herbaceous plant whose seeds are used as a spice. This species is native to Mediterranean regions and produces abundant yellow flowers, which mature into seed pods containing the small, spherical seeds from which yellow-coloured mustard is made (the darker mustards are made from seeds of other plants). This plant is mentioned in a rather puzzling metaphor in Matthew's gospel:

 ST MATTHEW
CH. 13, VV. 31-32

He told them another parable: "The kingdom of heaven is like a mustard seed, which a man took and planted in his field. Although it is the smallest of seeds, yet when it grows, it is the largest of garden plants and becomes a tree, so that the birds come and perch in its branches".

White mustard is unlikely to reach even a metre in height, so really does not qualify as

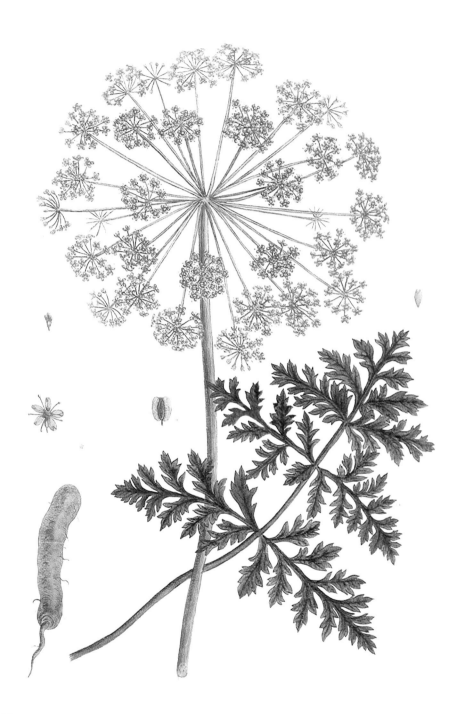

Dill

tree-like. However, relative to the size of its seeds it is a large plant, certainly taller than most others in the vegetable garden, and grows quickly too. Here it represents the Gospel, growing great from small beginnings, and offering shelter to the faithful.

Shortly before King David went to battle with Absolom, who had conspired against him, the people he was with

≈ 2 SAMUEL
CH. 17, vv. 28-29

brought wheat and barley, flour and roasted grain, beans and lentils, honey and curds, and cheese from cows' milk for David and his people to eat. ≈

It is suggested in *The Jewish Virtual Library* that the beans described in this passage were Broad Beans (*Vicia faba*); historians believe that this species was one of the earliest plants to be cultivated, and became part of mankind's diet in the eastern Mediterranean in around 6000 BC. Lentils (*Lens culinaris*) are small edible seeds in the pea family, also known as the legumes. This family of plants (Fabaceae) is notable in that most species have specialized nodules in their roots that hold populations of 'nitrogen-fixing' bacteria. The bacteria are able to extract atmospheric nitrogen, which is one of the elements necessary to build proteins, and use the nitrogen to form more complex carbon-based compounds, such as

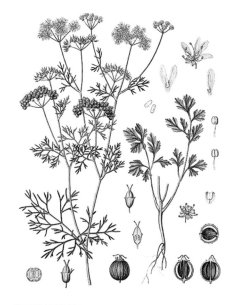

ammonia, which the plant can then use to form the complex proteins that make up its living tissues. In exchange for providing their host plants with a supply of protein 'building blocks', the bacteria receive sugars for food, these being made by the plant through the process of photosynthesis.

The seeds of the leguminous plants include peas and beans as well as lentils, and the group is known collectively as pulses. These have been eaten by humans since Neolithic times. Lentils were also one of the first crops cultivated in the Middle East, as long as 13,000 years ago. Modern science has discovered that they are a rich source of protein, a nutrient that can otherwise be hard to obtain from a mostly plant-based diet, and they were undoubtedly a very nutritionally important as well

CORIANDER

Broad Bean

as common food of poorer people, judging from the few references we have in the scriptures. When lentil pods are boiled they turn reddish-brown, still remembered by many today in the words of the *Authorized Version* as 'a mess of pottage'. The most famous Bible story which speaks of lentils is:

> *when Jacob was cooking some stew,*
> *Esau came in from the open country, famished.*
> *He said to Jacob* [his brother], *"Quick, let me*
> *have some of that red stew! I'm famished!"*
> *(That is why he was also called Edom).*
> *Jacob replied, "First sell me your birthright."*
> *"Look I am about to die" Esau said.*
> *"What good is the birthright to me?"*
> *But Jacob said, "Swear to me first." So he swore an*
> *oath to him, selling his birthright to Jacob.*
> *Then Jacob gave Esau some bread*
> *and some lentil stew.*

GENESIS
CH. 25, VV. 29-34

Later Jacob, encouraged by his mother, who treated Jacob as her favourite son, tricked his old, blind father into giving the eldest son's blessing to himself, causing much family friction. The two brothers were in fact fraternal twins, but it was Esau who was born first and should by rights have received the blessing. The story is a timely reminder even today of the dangers of parental favouritism.

One of the most exotic references to plants is in *Song of Songs*. The Lover says to his Beloved:

> *Your plants are an orchard of*
> *pomegranates and choice fruits,*
> *with henna and nard,*
> *nard and saffron,*
> *calamus and cinnamon,*
> *with every kind of incense tree,*
> *with myrrh and aloes*
> *and all the finest spices.*

SONG OF SONGS
CH. 4, VV. 13-14

WHITE MUSTARD

The substances named, all derived from various plants, are a mixture of fruits (discussed earlier in this chapter), cosmetics, spices and incense. Henna (*Lawsonia inermis*), or the Mignonette tree, 1.8–7.6 m (6–25 ft) tall, is found across Africa to Australia. The Lover mentions Henna early on in his praise of his beloved because she was certainly using Henna cosmetically. For more than 6,000 years the paste made from dried, crushed leaves mixed with one of several liquids has been used as a hair dye and as a paint to make intricate decorations on the skin. Mummies with red hair have been found in Ancient Egyptian tombs. At festivals such as Purim and Passover, use of henna was part of the Jewish celebrations. Some Jewish women have a henna party a week before a wedding, when the bride's grandmother paints the palms of the hands of the bride and groom-to-be as a blessing. The stain is a rich red-brown colour when used on the skin. It is also widely used today to colour hair, giving a glowing chestnut tint to darker hair, and colouring white or blonde hair a strikingly vivid red. We may picture the Beloved as a woman with beautiful henna-red hair, and henna tattoos on her skin.

Nard or spikenard is named only in *Song of Songs*. It is obtained from several plants, most commonly from a member of the valerian family (*Nardostachys jatamansi*). Prepared nard is an oil used as a perfume or as incense. It was probably the incense used in the Temple of Solomon and later, on the specialized incense altar (see the many references in Exodus and Leviticus, when the Hebrew Bible uses the word *HaKetoret*, 'the incense'). Much later it was part of the beginning of the story of the births of John the Baptist and his cousin Jesus Christ:

NARD

ST LUKE
CH. 1, VV. 8-9

Once when Zezhariah's division was on duty and
he was serving as priest before God, he was chosen
by lot, according to the custom of the priesthood, to
go into the temple of the Lord to burn incense.

The Angel Gabriel came to him as he stood by the incense altar and told him his wife would bear a son. Six months later the same angel visited Mary and told her she had been chosen by God to bear His son, Jesus. Nard was also a medicine to fight insomnia, birth difficulties and other minor ailments.

Cinnamon is mentioned as a spice at several points in the Bible, and so is cassia. Both terms probably relate to the same spice, obtained from the inner bark of trees of the genus *Cinnamomum* – today most commercially grown cinnamon comes from the tree *Cinnamomum cassia*. This sweet and distinctive spice is used as a flavouring in sweet and savoury foods in cuisines all around the world, and also in hot drinks. The tree itself is a fairly small evergreen. The bark is collected and rolled into 'cinnamon sticks' before it is dried out. These sticks are often added whole to a dish during slow cooking, which allows their sweet flavour to gradually infuse into the food.

The spice known as saffron was (and still is) a luxury item, derived from the Saffron Crocus (*Crocus sativus*), a cultivated form of the wild crocus of the Mediterranean region. It is used for flavouring and for imparting a vivid orange-yellow colour to food. The lilac-to-mauve flowers are harvested in the autumn. It is a notoriously expensive spice, because saffron powder is produced from freshly picked crocus flowers – but it comes only from the red stigmas or 'threads' that grow from the centres of the flowers, and each flower only produces three stigmas. These are parts of the flower's female reproductive system, adapted to receive pollen (produced by the plant's male reproductive parts, the stamens) and transport it to the flower's ovary where it will fertilize the seed. Only the stigmas in mature open flowers are suitable for saffron production.

To collect 450 g (1 lb) of dry saffron, you will need a harvest of 50,000–75,000 flowers. To produce a kilogram of the spice requires 110,000–170,000 flowers. The Beloved must have been a wealthy woman indeed, to have a farm and enough workers to be able to grow large numbers of crocuses and harvest enough stigmas for her saffron.

The Calamus or Sweet Flag (*Acorus calamus*) probably originated in Asia but is found widely in Europe. It is a wetland plant, whose scented leaves and even more strongly scented rhizomes (the plant's rootstock) have been used for many centuries in medicines, perfumes

Cinnamon

and as substitutes for ginger, cinnamon and nutmeg – which may be some of the other spices suggested by the Lover in the last line of the quotation on p. 85. We know that calamus was used as early as 1300 BC in Ancient Egypt. Its mention by the Lover may be most closely linked to its long having been a symbol of love, which was very much at the heart of his song. Elsewhere, it is mentioned once each in Isaiah (ch. 43, v. 24) and Jeremiah (ch. 6, v. 20), where it is most probably referred to as an ingredient in an anointing oil. Jeremiah clearly lists it as an imported item into Israel – 'from a distant land' – not a local product, again suggesting it was a luxury item for the Beloved to be growing.

The writer of Proverbs also mentions 'myrrh, aloes and cinnamon' together in one quotation (Proverbs ch. 7, v. 17). Myrrh was used as an ingredient in the embalming of bodies in Ancient Egypt, in sacred incense in the Temple, in the holy anointing oil (Esther ch. 2, v. 12) and as a drug to dull the senses. To Christians the last use is most famously mentioned as one of the three gifts given to Jesus at his birth by the Three Wise Men (St Matthew ch. 2, v. 11), and then in the drink offered to him by the Roman soldiers at His Crucifixion (St Mark ch. 15, v. 23).

Myrrh as described in the Bible is a resin, made from sap that is extracted from various small, very spiny trees of the genus *Commiphora*, in particular the species *Commiphora myrrha*. This species is often known simply as Myrrh, or African Myrrh, and is native to Arabia and eastern Africa. Its sap is collected by making cuts in the tree's bark and collecting the sap that leaks out – this soon coagulates into a hard resin. An oil can be distilled from the resin, and this is still used today in fragrances and medicines. A related species, *Commiphora gileadensis*, grows in the eastern Mediterranean. Whichever its source, myrrh is probably the 'balm' mentioned by the prophet Jeremiah as part of his cry of anguish: 'Is there no balm in Gilead?' (Jeremiah 8, v. 22). Gilead was the territory on the east side of the River Jordan just to the north of the Dead Sea. It was an important source of spices and was in the list of goods carried by the merchants who bought Joseph from his brothers (Genesis ch. 37, v. 25).

Aloes are succulent plants of many species, widespread across Africa, the Middle East and Asia. *Aloe vera* is the species most commonly used in herbal medicines. Its sap is used to produce a soothing ointment, to treat wounds and in the making of soap, and it is still used in the pharmaceutical industry today. The ancient Greeks and Romans, for example, used it to treat wounds. It is also increasingly used in a wide range of skin-soothing cosmetic products, and is marketed as a potent food supplement, effective at easing the symptoms of many different physical ailments (though rigorous scientific evidence of its efficacy is lacking). In eastern Asia, aloe-flavoured soft drinks and jelly-like puddings are popular.

SAFFRON CROCUS

In Romans, we find mention of another unpalatable plant:

He has filled me with bitter herbs;
And given me gall to drink.
He has broken my teeth with gravel;
He has trampled me in the dust.
I have been deprived of peace;
I have forgotten what prosperity is.

≫ ROMANS
CH. 8, VV. 18-31

So I say, 'My splendor is gone
And all that I had hoped from the Lord.
I remember my affliction and my wandering,
The bitterness and the gall.
I well remember them,
And my soul is downcast within me.
Yet this I call to mind,
And therefore I have hope …' ≫

The 'bitter herbs' could refer to any number of plants that people might try eating once, but perhaps not a second time. One possibility is the Endive (*Chichorium endivia*). It and the other endives, which are also known as chicory, have attractive daisy-like blue flowers, and lush leaf growth. The leaves look tempting and those who do not mind their bitter taste will enjoy the benefits of their high folate and vitamin A and K content. Bitter herbs of various kinds are also eaten on the night of Passover, in keeping with the commandment in Numbers ch. 9 v. 11: '… they are to do it on the fourteenth day of the second month at twilight. They are to eat the lamb, together with unleavened bread and bitter herbs.' The Hebrew term *maror* refers to these herbs, and at modern Passover suppers they include lettuce, endive and horseradish.

'Gall' is mentioned several times in the Bible in addition to the verse above, and refers to a drink flavoured with something bitter and unpleasant. However, this beverage is not necessarily intended to be given as a punishment or torment – a mixture of wine and gall was supposed to help ease the pain of the dying and make their transition to death easier to bear. For this reason, Jesus was offered this to drink when He was on the cross, by the handful of followers (including Mary, His mother and Mary Magdalene) who were present. When Jesus said He was thirsty, they soaked a sponge in the drink, then placed the sponge on a

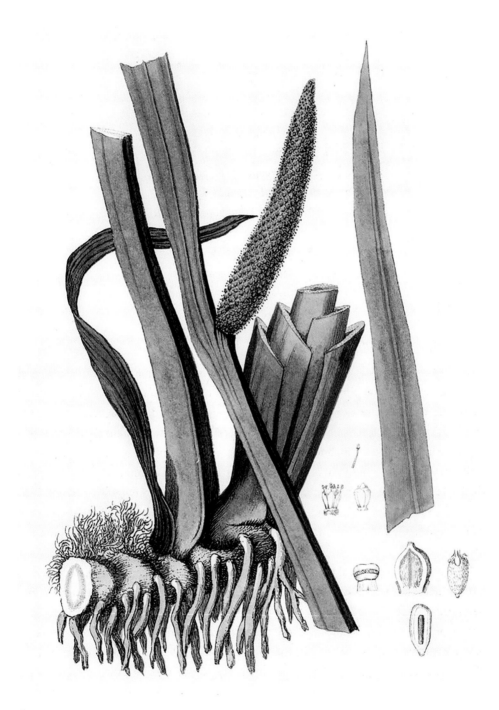

CALAMUS

ALOE VERA

long twig of hyssop – or possibly the leaves of the hyssop themselves were sufficient to collect up enough for a mouthful (see below for more about hyssop). They lifted it up to His face. In Mark's versions of the account, He drank the concoction and then died, but in Matthew's account He refused the pain relief, in an act of characteristic courage.

The plant that provided the bitter taste of gall could have been myrrh (see p. 89) but was possibly Wormwood (*Artemisia absinthium*). This perennial herb is widespread in temperate Eurasia and, as its name suggests, it is an ingredient of the powerfully intoxicating – and very bitter tasting – green spirit absinthe. Wormwood is mentioned by name, albeit with a somewhat different meaning, in a dramatic passage from Revelation:

REVELATION
CH. 8, VV. 10-11

The third angel sounded his trumpet, and a great star, blazing like a torch, fell from the sky on a third of the rivers and on the springs of water – the name of the star is Wormwood. A third of the waters turned bitter, and many people died from the waters that had become bitter.

This 'Wormwood' may have been a star rather than a plant, but it had the same effect of bringing bitterness. However, the plant wormwood is not typically toxic. It does contain a chemical that will cause death if consumed in very large quantities, but no human could eat enough of the plant to ingest a lethal dose of the chemical.

Finally, we consider the sacred plant Hyssop (*Hyssopus officinalis*), a member of the mint family, and native to southern Europe and the Middle East. It is used as an aromatic herb and as a medicine. This is a shrub with bright green foliage and sweet-scented flowers. It prefers warm and dry climates and

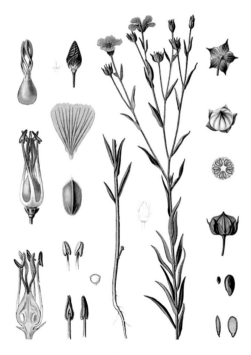

FLAX

WORMWOOD

sunny conditions, and its stems can be cut and dried in spring and again in autumn. Once dried, the leaves and flowers are removed. Dried hyssop has a minty taste and is often an ingredient in *za'atar*, a fragrant Middle Eastern spice blend that has begun to enjoy great popularity in other countries since the turn of the century. It is also used to produce an essential oil, which has antiseptic properties.

This is the plant known as hyssop today, but in the Bible stories of religious rituals, another species of mint – one with a straight stalk and a hairy surface to its leaves which hold liquids well – is sometimes considered to be a better contender. This is *Origanum syriacum* or *O. maru*, popularly known as the Bible Hyssop. Whichever species is involved, the first biblical mention of hyssop is a dramatic one, in the time leading up to the Israelites leaving Egypt:

⇆ EXODUS
CH. 11, vv. 31-13

Then Moses summoned all the elders of Israel and said to them, "Go at once and select the animals for your families and slaughter the Passover lamb. Take a bunch of hyssop, dip it into the blood in the basin and put some of the blood in the top and on both sides of the door frame. Not one of you shall go out of the door of his house until morning. When the Lord goes through the land to strike down the Egyptians he will see the blood on the top and sides of the door frame and will pass over the doorway, and he will not permit the destroyer to enter your houses and strike you down." ⇆

Later, a law was made which said that a person who had suffered an infectious disease could be cleansed by sprinkling him or her with blood from a slaughtered bird, which was on the tip of a sprig of hyssop (Leviticus ch. 14, vv. 1–9). Given the known antiseptic properties of *Hyssopus officinalis*, this method may have been effective, if this was indeed the herb described. Any success, though, would have been in spite of rather than because of the sprinkling of avian blood, which was surely an unnecessary part of the process from a medical point of view. However, it certainly had a symbolic relevance. The writer of *The letter to the Hebrews* firmly reminds his readers of this use of the hyssop stick when he writes about the blood of Christ, and declares:

HYSSOP

 HEBREWS
CH. 9, V. 9

In fact, the law requires that nearly everything be cleansed with blood, and without the shedding of blood there is no forgiveness.

Today Christians celebrate this in the sacrament of Holy Communion, the Eucharist, when they eat the bread and drink the wine, the body and blood of Christ, in remembrance of His taking the sins of the world on His shoulders (1 Corinthians ch. 11, vv. 23–26).

CHAPTER III

FLOWERS

There is much in the news nowadays about the land around the world and what grows on it – or does not grow, because we have ruined the ground with pesticides, or have built on it, or caused severe erosion through deforestation. It is of concern to many people. About 11 per cent of our planet's land surface is currently used for cultivation of some kind – but only 36 per cent of the planet's total land area is actually suitable for the purpose. There are vast tracts of land – desert, mountainside, tundra and human habitation – where the range of plants that will grow is extremely limited. As our population expands, so the area of land available for us to grow the food we need – never mind the land needed by all of the other species sharing our world – continues to shrink. Our methods of cultivation often do lasting damage to the land as well.

In the United Kingdom the authorities are increasingly aware of the way that wild flowers show us the state of health of the land, and are helping landowners to farm profitably in an ecofriendly way. But not all the people involved will believe that God had a hand in what they do, when He declared:

 GENESIS
CH. 1, VV. 26-31

"Let us make man in our image, in our likeness,
and let them rule over the fish of the sea and
the birds of the air, over the livestock,
over all the earth. And over all the creatures
that move along the ground."
So God created man in his own image ...
Then God said, "I give you every seed-bearing
plant on the face of the whole earth and every
tree that has fruit with seed in it" ... And God saw
all that he had made, and it was very good. ≈

So God made humankind the rulers of all other life on Earth, but it is all too easy to forget that any role of this nature should be about guardianship, as much as it is about dominion. We have certainly become an overwhelmingly dominant force on Earth, but our care of our land and the abundance of life it supports, over the millennia, has left a great deal to be desired. The Bible does make a point about this responsibility. There is much debate about that gift of all those plants, and the statement which followed:

GENESIS
CH. 2, V. 15

The Lord God took the man and put him in the Garden of Eden to work it and take care of it.

Many people of different faiths *do* still believe that they have to *take care of* the land and what grows there. That is the very nature of how they 'rule over' it. They have lived long on the land, and have grown to realize that as a family or tribe or nation they have lived long because they do realize how best to look after the farm or the forest. If they are greedy or careless, they will grow hungry, or starve and die. St Peter wrote a letter in the early 60s AD, which he addressed to the gentile Christians in particular, who were spread across Asia Minor. In their time of Roman oppression, he reminded them of the steadfastness of God when they felt downtrodden, by quoting words that the prophet Isaiah had said to the Israelites centuries before:

1 PETER
CH. 1, VV. 23-25

&

ISAIAH
CH. 40, VV. 6-8

For you have been born again, not of perishable seed, but of imperishable, through the living and enduring word of God. For,
All men are like grass,
and all their glory like the flowers of the field;
the grass withers and the flowers fall,
but the word of the Lord stands for ever.

Let us consider in some detail the 'grass' and the 'flowers' that the writers record on and off throughout the Bible. We dismiss many plants in the countryside, and more so if they are in our gardens, as 'weeds'. To a gardener, trying to cultivate a display of showy flowers, a weed is any wild plant (although most often an unattractive and fast-growing one) that has taken up space intended for the fancy flowers. To a farmer, wild plants growing too prolifically in his crop fields could have a devastating impact on his income and on the food supplies of the whole neighbourhood. As such, weeds are not to be tolerated at all, either in the garden or on the farm. The word is used repeatedly in the Parable of the Weeds, which is recorded only in St Matthew's gospel:

Jesus told them another parable: "The kingdom of heaven is like a man who sowed good seed in his field. But while everyone was sleeping, his enemy came and sowed weeds among the wheat, and went away. Then the wheat sprouted and formed ears, then the weeds also appeared.
The owner's servants came to him and said, "Sir, didn't you sow good seed in your field? Where then did the weeds come from?"
"An enemy did this", he replied.

His disciples did not understand the parable and Jesus had to explain it to them. He was the landowner, the Devil was the enemy, the field was the world and the weeds were the sons of the Devil; and at harvest time, the end of the age, angels will weed out the kingdom and throw the evil into the fire, and the righteous will be gathered to be with their father. The old translations used the word 'tares' for the weeds, and many commentators now believe the weed was the grass Darnel (*Lolium temulentum*), also known as Cockle. It grows where wheat is grown, and looks so like it that it is also called false wheat. Not until the ears appear can the two be easily separated: ripe wheat ears are brown, but those of Darnel are black. The similarity between wheat and Darnel before this is so great that the ancient Greek botanist Theophrastus stated that sown wheat could literally transform into Darnel as it grew.

The seeds of Darnel can be infected with a fungus. Some herbivorous animals such as cattle seem able to eat the infected seeds without ill-effect, but if they are eaten by humans they can cause a drunken nausea or even

DARNEL

death – the scientific name *temulentum* means 'drunk'. Jesus really did know about the problems of harvest time. His message would have been much more dramatic to his hearers than to us when we hear just the word 'weeds'.

For centuries before the Star of David became a well-known Jewish symbol, the seven-branched lampstand called the 'menorah' was the best-known symbol. Its form was described by God to Moses as part of God's instructions for the building of the Tabernacle and its furnishings:

 EXODUS
CH. 25, VV. 31-32

Make a lampstand of pure gold and hammer it out, base and shaft; its flower-like cups, buds and blossoms shall be of one piece with it. Six branches are to extend from the sides of the lampstand – three on one side and three on the other. ≈

Although the cups for the oil lamps on top of each branch are described as being 'like almond flowers', there is an ancient Jewish tradition that suggests that the shape of the complete lamp resembles the flower they call 'moriah', or 'morvah', which botanists know as the Jerusalem Sage or Jerusalem Salvia (*Salvia hierosolymitana*). This is a native plant of the area, in the same family as mint. Jerusalem Sage is drought resistant, and lights up the stony landscape in spring with its pink flowers. It is not to be confused with *Phlomis fruticosa*, another species that sometimes goes by the English name Jerusalam Sage. *P. fruticosa*, native to the Mediterranean region, is a small evergreen shrub that produces distinctive whorls of bright yellow flowers.

There are two other related flowers, the Pungent or Dominican Sage (*Salvia dominica*) and Land of Israel Sage or Palestine Sage (*S. palaestina*) to be found commonly in the Holy Land. While the Jerusalem Sage has vivid, deep pink flowers, the other two species produce white or pale pink flowers, but all have the same attractive shape, with a tubular corolla, a projecting lower 'lip' surmounted by a hood. This flower form is common to all members of the mint family but most have very small flowers, with only a few having such large and showy blooms as these three *Salvia* species. All three may have had an influence on the designs of the cups – indeed, one commentator has said they are 'menorahs growing wild'.

All three of these sage species can be seen growing in the 400-acre Neot Kedumim – the Biblical Landscape Reserve in Israel, halfway between Jerusalem and Tel Aviv. This remarkable series of gardens, covering 625 acres, is being specially constructed to show all the plants named in the Bible. With regular exhibitions and workshops as well as space to freely explore its landscapes, the park is a haven for Bible scholars and botanists alike.

At Neot Kedumin, the 'menorah plants' all grow in a terrace at the top of the hill. The gardens' emblem is an opened flower of the Caper (*Capparis spinosa*), a plant which is mentioned only once in the Bible – if you believe some translations, such as this one from the *British Revised Version*:

> ✑ ECCLESIASTES   *... the grasshopper loses its spring,*
> CH. 12, V. 5   *and the caper berry has no effect;* ✑

Although this is clearly the flower named in the Septuagint (Greek), the Vulgate (Latin) and a few modern English versions, most translations, such as the widely read *New International Version*, the *Revised King James* and the *Good News Bible*, have the word 'desire' instead of 'the caper berry'. The founders of the gardens believe the caper's productivity, strength and endurance are all what is meant by modern 'Israel'. However, in biblical times the plant was believed to have aphrodisiac properties, so we are back to 'desire' again.

The caper is an attractive shrub that grows around the Mediterranean, and prefers dry

climates. Today the caper is well known for its edible flower buds, which are collected and preserved in vinegar, for use as a seasoning. These buds, which are often known simply as 'capers', are used particularly in southern Italian cuisine, adding their intense peppery flavour to pasta sauces. However, they are also one of the key ingredients of tartar sauce, which is most likely to be found alongside a plate of fish and chips in a British seaside restaurant. If the buds are left on the plant, they open out as dramatically pretty flowers, with large white petals and a mass of dangling, purple-tipped stamens. The ripe green berries of the caper are also edible, and tend to be preserved in vinegar, like miniature olives.

JERUSALEM SAGE

The heart-warming story of how Joseph saved Egypt and his family from starving in a time of famine by carefully storing the grain from several good harvests (see p. 72), is followed by tales of the oppressed lives the Israelites lived in Egypt until they were led to freedom by Moses. His life began very dramatically after the Pharaoh had shown concern about the number of Israelites being born in his kingdom. The Pharaoh decreed that all newborn boys should be thrown into the Nile River. Moses's mother managed to hide him for three months after his birth but then put him in a papyrus basket coated with tar and pitch and put it in the reeds on the banks of the Nile.

The happy result was that Moses was rescued by an Egyptian princess. Historians believe she may have been Hatshepsut, 'Foremost of noble ladies', who became queen and later Pharaoh. She oversaw a great many building projects, including that of an amazing temple near Luxor, and died in 1458 BC after a 19-year reign. Even more intriguing for the purpose of this chapter is the description of the basket, which gives us the well-known story 'Moses and the bullrushes'. What plants are mentioned? Papyrus and reeds. The Papyrus (*Cyperus papyrus*) is a wetland sedge that grows along the Nile, in swampy flooded areas. It is a strikingly tall sedge, reaching up to 5 m (16 ft) in height, with long, sturdy stems that sprout from its woody rhizome. Each stem supports a large cluster of thinner, bright green stems that sprout off from the crown in all directions, giving the plant the appearance of a firework frozen in time (or, more prosaically, a feather duster).

Papyrus was used by the Ancient Egyptians as far back as the fourth millennium BC. The pith of its stems was soaked, cut into lengths, beaten and fixed together to make a sheet that when dry could be written on, then rolled into a scroll to be stored. Papyrus documents as old as 2500 BC have been discovered at a site on the Red Sea coast. Even more interesting is the following prophecy:

ISAIAH
CH. 18, VV. 1-2

Woe to the land of whirring wings
along the rivers of Cush [ancient Ethiopia],
which sends envoys by sea
in papyrus boats over the water.

The stems and leaves of papyrus were durable enough to be woven into a strong basket, or even a boat. The mention of reeds in the story of Moses is a mistranslation. The writers of the *Authorized Version* were not familiar with vegetation along the Nile and translated the ancient word with the name of a plant that seemed right to them – the general word 'reeds',

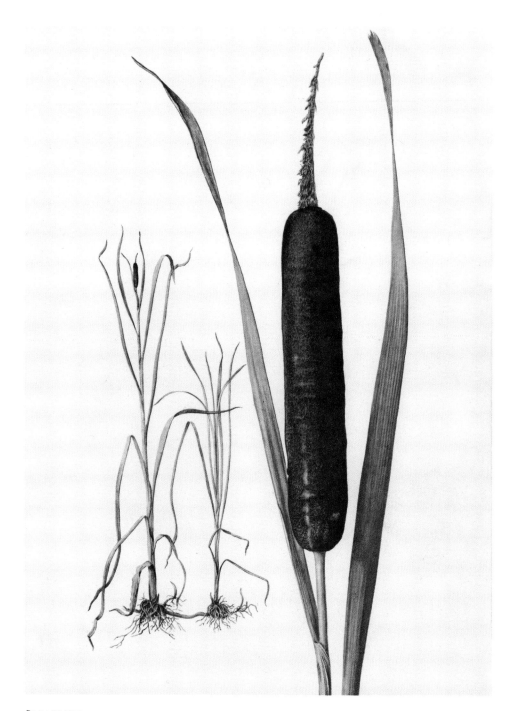

Bullrush

after the reedbed-forming wetland grasses of the genus *Phragmites*, especially the Common Reed (*Phragmites australis*), and the Bullrush or Reedmace (*Typha latifolia*). Both common reeds and bullrushes are familiar sights alongside English rivers. However, the Hebrew word here, *gime,* really refers to papyrus. The idea of Moses in the bullrushes really stuck in the modern mind due to the frequent depiction of the story by artists showing English bullrushes with their distinctive sausage-shaped seed-heads, despite there being many paintings from previous centuries that clearly show a different plant, native to the Nile – the Papyrus. (However, it is worth pointing out that you will also find representatives of both *Phragmites* and *Typha* growing in profusion in the delta lakes of the Nile.)

Another problem in translation is that concerned with the Bible's mentions of thorns, briars, thistles, nettles and brambles. Modern scholarship is certain about the species identity of some of these, but not all. For example, the prophet Isaiah had comforting words for the Israelites in exile:

Seek the Lord while he may be found;
call on him while he is near.
You will go out in joy
and be led forth in peace;
ISAIAH *the mountains and hills*
CH. 55, v.v 6 & 12-13 *will burst into song before you,*
and all the trees of the field
will clap their hands.
Instead of the thornbush will grow the pine tree.
And instead of briers the myrtle will grow.

As we have seen (p. 19) the thorns could be those on the acacia bush. However, the brier (more usually spelt 'briar' today) is also mentioned by Job, who in his anger, curses his land:

JOB *then let briers come up instead of wheat*
CH. 31, v. 40 *and weeds instead of barley.*

The *Zondervan Encyclopedia of the Bible* records that the Hebrew word here, *hoah*, is one of several in the language used for thorns. Job's curse appears in the *Revised Standard Version* of the Bible as 'foul weeds'. The *Encyclopedia* wonders whether the plant could be the

Palestinian Nightshade

Palestinian Nightshade (*Solanum incanum*), which is a common weed in the Jordan valley, and native to the Middle East. It is a member of the nightshade family and is related to the two species found in Britain; like them, it has poisonous berries. It certainly is not the wild Sweetbriar Rose or Eglantine (*Rosa rubiginosa*) that grows in British hedgerows. Whatever plant was originally meant, and whichever English word is in the translation, it is clear that

THISTLE

a plant with disagreeable features is meant because of the contrast made between it and the Myrtle (*Myrtus communis*), which as discussed earlier (see p. 37) was a prized plant indeed. The myrtle has aromatic leaves and white flowers from which spices and medicines were made, it is named as one of God's blessings and its twigs are still used in the ritual of the Feast of the Booths.

Thorns feature prominently in one of Jesus's parables, recorded in St Matthew ch. 13, St Mark ch. 4 and St Luke ch. 8: 'The Parable of the Sower'. Thistles (*Centaurea* species) are also used as an image of misery. Several species of thistle can be found growing on the rough ground of the hills around Galilee. They are extremely valuable nectar sources for all kinds of insects, but the people of biblical times had little use for them. The *Good News Bible* translates the Job passage we have just mentioned as '... then

ACANTHUS SYRIACUS

instead of wheat and barley, may weeds and thistles grow', and three times Isaiah warns that the Israelites will be punished by God, as when he says, for example, 'The wickedness of the people burns like a fire that destroys thorn-bushes and thistles' (Isaiah ch. 9, v. 18). The *NIV* translation is not so precise; the fire 'consumes briers and thorns'. Amaziah, King of Judah, was at war with Jehoash, King of Israel, in the late 700s BC, and:

≈ 2 CHRONICLES
CH. 25, VV. 17-18

When Amaziah king of Judah consulted his advisors, he sent this challenge to Jehoash son of Jehoahaz, son of Jehu, king of Israel: "Come, meet me face to face".
But Jehoash king of Israel replied to Amaziah king of Judah: "A thistle in Lebanon sent a message to a cedar in Lebanon, 'Give my daughter to my son in marriage.' Then a wild beast in Lebanon came along and trampled the thistle underfoot." ≈

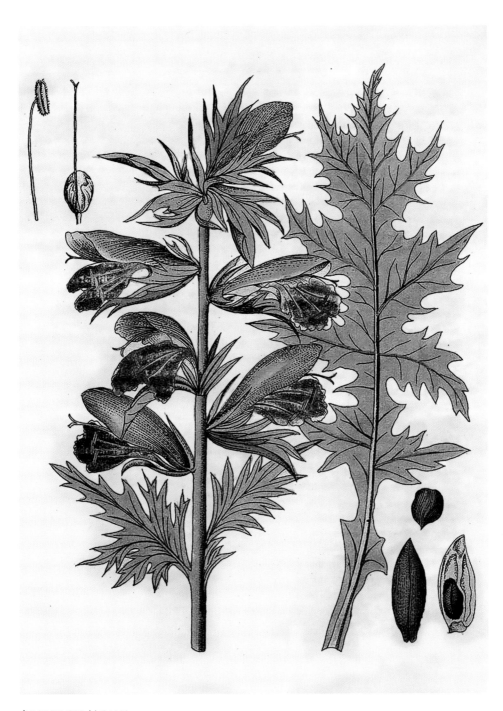

ACANTHUS MOLLIS

It has already already been mentioned (see p. 22) how great in many respects the cedar tree was. How insignificant a thistle would appear beside such a tree. Jehoash, the 'wild beast', did rout the Amaziah thistle in battle shortly afterwards. The meaning is clear in the references to a thistle, as anyone can appreciate who has been out walking and has brushed against the prickly stems of a thistle, or tried to pick one of its lovely flowers, and cried aloud with pain.

(see p. 22)

Another mention of briers comes in Isaiah ch. 55, v. 13: 'Instead of the thornbush will grow the juniper, and instead of briers the myrtle will grow. This will be for the Lord's renown, for an everlasting sign, that will endure forever.' The replacement of thornbushes with juniper trees represents hopefulness, but the young foliage of junipers (*Juniperus* species) is still very dense and thorny, and not pleasant to tangle with. However, the juniper also bears strongly flavoured berries, used as a flavouring, and this compensates somewhat for its prickliness. Today, the most common use for juniper berries is as a key flavouring for gin, and indeed the word 'gin' is derived from the Dutch word for juniper (*jenever*).

SCARLET
MARTAGON

Despite the ministrations of his Comforter, Bildad, Job bemoans the way he is treated by the young sons of men who were forced to live rough:

JOB
CH. 30, V. 7
(AUTHORIZED VERSION)

Among the bushes they brayed;
under the nettles they were gathered together.

There are no Stinging Nettles (*Urtica dioica*) in modern translations, just men 'huddled in the undergrowth'. It is hard to imagine anyone lying in a bed of nettles without suffering greatly. The nettles of the Bible may not have been this species in any case. The plant *Acanthus mollis*, which goes by a variety of common names, including bear's breeches, sea dock, bear's foot plant, sea holly and oyster plant, is another possible candidate, as is the related *A. syriacus*. These are sturdy herbaceous perennials that grow mainly in coastal areas in the Mediterranean region. In full flower, they are very beautiful (certainly much more striking than a stinging nettle), with a tall stem of large pale pink or white flowers, each with a dark red or green sepal as a hood. Their leaves are holly-like in appearance, and *A. syriacus* is rather prickly, but *A. mollis* is not (*mollis* means 'soft'). Decorative representations of

Acanthus leaves can be found in Corinthian architecture, adorning the tops or 'capitals' of pillars in grand buildings.

The last of the prickly plants is the Bramble (*Rubus fruticosus*) – at least, that is the species we affectionately know and harvest wild or cultivated as the blackberry. This is a genetically complex plant with numerous varieties, and we cannot be sure which one St Luke was referring to here in recording these words of Jesus:

> *No good tree bears bad fruit, nor does a bad tree*
> *bear good fruit. Each tree is recognized by its own*
> *fruit. People do not pick figs from thorn-bushes,*
>
> **ST LUKE** *or grapes from briers. A good man brings forth*
> CH. 6, VV. 43-45 *good things out of the good stored up in his heart,*
> *and an evil man brings evil things out of the evil*
> *stored up in his heart. For out of the overflow*
> *of his heart his mouth speaks.*

The *Good News Bible* boldly says 'bramble bushes' not 'briers'. Jesus uses images from the countryside several times. He was often alone in the hills, so would have been familiar with briers or brambles. The ones He knew well and believed His audience would recognize, were not ones that gave good fruit like we know, but were plants that were useless as food, so underlining His comparison of good and evil, which is what He was preaching about.

The last group of plants comprises those we would acknowledge as flowers as opposed to weeds. Jesus's well-known words to His disciples set the scene:

> *Consider how the lilies grow. They do not labour or*
> *spin. Yet I tell you, not even Solomon in all his*
>
> **ST LUKE** *splendour was dressed like one of these. If that is*
> CH. 12, VV. 27-29 *how God clothes the grass of the field, which is here*
> *today, and tomorrow is thrown into the fire, how*
> *much more will he clothe you, O you of little faith!*

The lilies spoken of in the New Testament by St Luke were recorded by the Greek word *krinia*. They may be the Scarlet Martagon (*Lilium chalcedonicum*) or Red Turk's-cap Lily, which Balfour in his *Plants of the Bible* (1886) says 'comes into flower at the season of the

CYCLAMEN

year when our Lord's sermon on the mount is supposed to have been delivered. It is abundant in the district of Galilee; and its fine scarlet flowers render it a very conspicuous and showy object, which would naturally attract the attention of the hearers.'

We cannot, of course, be certain that 'lilies' literally meant members of the lily family, and some translations of the verse substitute 'wild flowers' for 'lilies'. Some commentators, however, do strongly argue that the word, in both the Old and New Testaments, would have denoted liliaceous plants in general. However, it could refer to another plant family, the irises and their cousins, and in particular the genus *Iris*, which is 'large, vigorous, elegant in form and gorgeous in colouring'. Another possible identity for St Luke's lilies is the Cyclamen (*Cyclamen hederifolium*). The flowers of this member of the primrose family are attractive indeed, bearing five large pink, purple or white petals that stand upright and have unusual rippling edges. Yet another possibility are lupins (*Lupinus* species), which are attractive relatives of the broom (see p. 93). In all likelihood, Jesus was asking His disciples to consider all wild flowers, in their varied and beautiful profusion.

The *Concordance to the Good News Bible* lists nearly 40 references for 'flower', but few that give the actual name of a particular type of flower. Even when the flower type is more or less specified, there is often disagreement in other translations. For example, the prophet Hosea at the end of his book tells of God's promise to bring a blessing to Israel:

HOSEA
CH. 14, vv. 4-5 (NIV)

I will heal their waywardness
and love them freely,
for my anger has turned away from them.
I will be like the dew to Israel;
he will blossom like a lily.

But *NIV's* 'blossom like a lily' becomes 'blossom like flowers' in *The Good News*.

In the Old Testament the Hebrew name *shushan* or *shoshan*, that is 'whiteness', was used as the general name for several plants common to the eastern Mediterranean, such as the tulip, iris, anemone, gladiolus and buttercup. Some interpret the 'blossoming lily', with much probability, as denoting the Water-lily (*Nymphoea lotus*) or Lotus. Its flowers are large, and they are white with streaks of pink. They supplied models for the ornaments of the pillars of Solomon's temple (1 Kings ch. 7, v. 19).

A different point of view was held by the Rev. Tristram, who wrote *The Natural History of the Bible* (1867), in which he describes some of the true 'floral glories of Palestine', including

ANEMONE

'the Pheasant's Eye (*Adonis palestina*), the Persian Buttercup (*Ranunuculus asiaticus*) and the Anemone (*Anemone coronaria*). The last named is, however, with the greatest probability regarded as the 'lily of the field' to which our Lord refers.'

'Certainly,' continued the Rev. Tristram (who had spent much time in the region in question, and so should know) 'if, in the wondrous richness of bloom which characterizes the land of Israel in spring, any one plant can claim pre-eminence, it is the Anemone, the most natural flower for our Lord to pluck and seize upon as an illustration, whether walking in the fields or sitting on the hill-side. The White Water-lily (*Nymphcea alba*) and the Yellow Water-lily (*Nuphar lutea*) are both abundant in the marshes of the Upper Jordan, but have no connection with the lily of Scripture.'

Whatever the flower, or flowers, referred to in these verses, their symbolic meaning is usually fairly clear. In the case of Luke ch. 12, vv. 27–29, Jesus is pointing out that Solomon's glory is artificial, organized and dressed by Solomon himself, whereas the disciples – and we – should cast all our care upon the Lord.

The Beloved and the Lover in their duet say – or sing – to each other:

Beloved
I am a rose of Sharon,
a lily of the valleys.

 SONG OF SONGS
CH. 2, VV. 1-2

Lover
Like a lily among thorns
is my darling among the maidens.

Sharon is the coastal plain south of Mt Carmel. 'Rose of Sharon' first appeared in English in the 1611 *Authorized King James Bible*, and has since become a name around the world for many different beautiful flowers. For example, a *Hibiscus* Rose of Sharon is the national flower of South Korea. Various scholarly attempts have been published to say which 'rose' it is; they are all certain it is not one of the true roses (*Rosa* species) that we know. It has been suggested that it is a mistranslation of a general Hebrew word for crocus; it might be the red Mountain Tulip (*Tulipa montana*), which is common in the hills around Sharon; or perhaps it is most likely that it is the white Sea Daffodil (*Pancratium maritimum*), which is common around the shores of the Mediterranean.

The lovers seem to be trying to outdo each other with compliments. The loving couple are

SEA DAFFODIL

both picturing the woman as white, in some symbolic sense, even though it is clear from other verses that her skin is dark ('Dark am I, yet lovely, daughters of Jerusalem, dark like the tents of Kedar, like the tent curtains of Solomon'). The colour white often represents purity; this symbolic link may be emphasized in the man's choice of 'lily' – the impressive Madonna Lily (*Lilium candidum*), perhaps, which is native to the area? It is not clear whether the Beloved is describing herself as two distinctly different flowers, or whether 'rose of sharon' and 'lily of the valleys' should be taken as synonymous.

The Paperwhite Narcissus (*Narcissus tazetta*) is also sometimes known as the Chinese Sacred Lily, and this flower could also be a 'lily of the valleys'. It has a very broad distribution, including the Mediterranean as well as all the way east to China, and is a conspicuous, attractive and indeed mostly white flower. Unlike the majority of daffodils and narcissi, it bears several flowers on each stem, giving rise to another name of Bunch-flowered Daffodil. The flowers have the typical daffodil shape, with a central ring or short tube of fused orange petals surrounded by six much larger, separate white petals.

HYACINTH

Yet another possible 'lily of the valleys' that is not actually a lily is the Hyacinth (*Hyacinthus orientalis*). This gorgeous flower is native to western Asia, including parts of the Holy Land. In Britain we know it as a garden flower, which may be white, cream, dark red, various shades of pink or purple, or vivid violet-blue – the latter is the natural colour of its wild ancestor, but white forms may occur spontaneously in the wild as well as in cultivation. Hyacinths flower in late winter, providing a reminder of spring to come, and have a delightful sweet fragrance. The hyacinth flower shares its name with a kind of reddish gemstone, a form of zircon. Another name for this gem is 'jacinth', and it is mentioned by name (and substituted for hyacinth in some translations) in Revelation, as the constituent of one of the twelve foundational stones of New Jerusalem:

> ≫ REVELATION
> CH. 21, V. 20

> *the fifth onyx, the sixth ruby, the seventh chrysolite,*
> *the eighth beryl, the ninth topaz,*
> *the tenth turquoise, the eleventh jacinth,*
> *and the twelfth amethyst.* ≫

Madonna Lily

Perhaps the most unusual plant-related occurrence recorded in the Bible is found in the story of Jacob's wife, Rachel. When she learns that her sister, Leah, is pregnant she is jealous. Then:

GENESIS
CH. 30, vv. 14-16

During wheat harvest, Reuben went out into the fields and found some mandrake plants, which he brought to his mother Leah. Rachel said to Leah, "Please give me some of your son's mandrakes." But she said to her, "Wasn't it enough that you took away my husband? Will you take my son's mandrakes too?" "Very well," Rachel said, "he can sleep with you tonight in return for your son's mandrakes." So when Jacob came in from the fields that evening, Leah went out to meet him. "You must sleep with me," she said. "I have hired you with my son's mandrakes." So he slept with her that night.

Jacob had fled to his uncle Laban after he had tricked his own father and obtained his brother's birthright. He fell in love with Rachel, Laban's beautiful daughter, but was tricked himself by Laban and found himself married to Leah, the older, weak-eyed sister. In the end, Leah was the mother of most of Jacob's 12 sons, although eventually Jacob took Rachel as a second wife and she was the mother of his youngest two sons, one of whom was the famous Joseph (see p. 71). Read Genesis chapters 28–30 for the whole story.

An Israelite man in theory could have several wives. The Bible explicitly allowed a man to have more than one wife. God gives Moses a law that talks about making sure the first wife still gets the same resources and attention even after she has ceased to be the only one, Exodus ch. 21, vv. 10–11. So in Jacob's time, what happened to him and Leah was not an improper act as many will see it today.

The mandrake is the common name for several species of the genus *Mandragora* of the nightshade family. The most likely species here is *Mandragora officinarum*. The forked, fleshy roots of the plant are also known as mandrakes. In shape, they often resemble the torso and limbs of a human body, and for this reason they have strong links to various

Mandrake

superstitions in different parts of the world, and have a role in pagan traditions. One of the ideas associated with them is that, if eaten, they can help a woman become pregnant. The Hebrew word for it is *doo-dah'-ee*, meaning literally 'love-producing'. The roots are hallucinogenic and narcotic. The Beloved just discussed is not such an innocent as she seemed earlier when she says to her Lover:

Let us go early to the vineyards
to see if the vines have budded,
if their blossoms have opened,
SONG OF SONGS *and if the pomegranates are in bloom –*
CH. 7, V. 12-13 *there I will give you my love.*
The mandrakes send out their fragrance
and at our door is every delicacy, both new and old,
that I have stored up for you, my lover.

The Song of Songs, and the tale of Jacob, Leah and Rachel, would be amazing soap-opera stories by our standards. Life carries on much as it has done for centuries.

FURTHER READING

Alter, R.	2010	*The Wisdom Books – Job, Proverbs and Ecclesiastes*
Baly, D.	1959	*The Geography of the Bible*
Beer, E.	2007	*Flora and Fauna of the Bible* (mostly pictures)
Bouquet, A. C.	1953	*Everyday Life in New Testament Times*
Fish, H. D.	1998	*Animals of the Bible* (with Caldecott Medal winning illustrations by D. P. Lathrop)
Goodfellow, P.	2015	*Fauna and Flora of the Bible – a Guide for Bible Readers and Naturalists*
Hareuveni, N. with Frenkley, H.	1988	*Ecology in the Bible* (2nd edn).
Hastings, J. (ed.).	1909	10th impression, 1946. *Dictionary of the Bible*
Heaton, E. W	1956	*Everyday Life in Old Testament Times*
Moldenke, H. & Moldenke, A	2005	*Plants of the Bible*
Reid, C.	1993	*Berlitz: Discover Israel*
Swenson, A. A.	1995	*Plants of the Bible and How to Grow Them*
Tristram, Rev. H. B.	1884	*Fauna and Flora of Palestine*

All Bible quotations are from *The NIV Study Bible: New International Version* (1998 edition) of the International Bible Society, unless otherwise stated.

Other Bible quotations about the plants and animals we have studied can be found at several websites, including International Standard Bible Encyclopedia, the Jewish Virtual Library, the McClintock and Strong Biblical Cyclopedia, ChristianAnswers.net, biblestudytools.com and the Holman Bible Dictionary.

INDEX